Law Enforcement Families
THE ULTIMATE BACKUP

Bob —
    Your endorsement of this
book is valued and appreciated.
I thank you sincerely for
your unconditional friendship
for the past two decades.
I wish your family
continued happiness.

                        Jim
                        12/7/07

ADVANCE PRAISE FOR LAW ENFORCEMENT FAMILIES THE ULTIMATE BACKUP

"The book should be required reading for every officer, deputy, and their loved ones. Law Enforcement Families: The Ultimate Backup will become to the law enforcement profession what Gray's Anatomy has been to the field of medicine."

Barbara Morris, spouse of Sheriff Charles W. Morris, Okaloosa County, Florida

"In law enforcement, we are always aware of our surroundings and the dangers that lurk therein. The hardest thing for cops to do is look for that danger inside themselves. This book begs us to look in the mirror, whether we want to or not!"

Sergeant Mike Peruggia, New York Police Department EAP

"Relationships will be enhanced with these truths and reminders. An engaging book, taking the reader to that unique place where resolute souls and law enforcement family members commit and sacrifice for the sake of society."

Robert Kelly, Supervisory Special Agent, FBI Retired

Law Enforcement Families
THE ULTIMATE BACKUP

James T. Reese, PHD
Cherie Castellano CSW, LPC

© 2007 James T. Reese, PhD, and Cherie Castellano, LPC

ISBN 978-0-9799676-0-3

Library of Congress Control Number: 2007907644

LAW ENFORCEMENT FAMILIES: The Ultimate Backup

All Scripture quotations are taken from the Holy Bible, King James Version, published by the International Bible Association, Dallas, TX, 1974.

Edited by Rich Cairnes of Goofproof Proof (rich@goofproofproof.com)
Cover design by GFO Designs
Printed in the United States of America

Published by Richmond Hill Press LLC
100 Richmond Hill
Williamsburg, VA 23185-3948   USA

DEDICATION

Records prove that laws have been, since the beginning of time, created and enforced by the inhabitants of this Earth for the safety of mankind. While the responsibilities, duties, and scope of enforcing these laws has changed monumentally, the purpose of law enforcement, and police work in general, remains the same: TO SERVE AND PROTECT. In order to do this effectively, all the elements of an officer's support system are put to the test. Each day they are asked to be patient, unwearied, uncomplaining, enduring, brave, tolerant, forgiving, forbearing, sympathetic, understanding, and supportive. This book is dedicated to law enforcement families in every free society, all of whom try to exhibit all these traits and qualities, everyday. Dedicating this book to them is our attempt to publicly acknowledge their importance.

TABLE OF CONTENTS

ACKNOWLEDGMENTS

No part of this book would have been possible, nor any chapter in it valid, without the genuine and honest information provided by police officers and their families. We also wish to acknowledge the assistance of thousands of law enforcement chaplains, counselors, and clinicians who, throughout the years, have provided these authors with their honest feelings, cautions, and concerns about the hazards facing officers and their families.

The authors are most grateful to those who are first in their lives: Dr. Reese's wife, Sandra, their daughter, Jamie Reese Baker, and her husband, Bryan Baker; Mrs. Castellano's husband, Detective Supervisor Mark Castellano, and their sons, Domenick and Louis John. Louis and Bernadette Terminello have offered Mrs. Castellano assistance in this book and in life, for which she expresses her thanks. Our mission in completing this book never would have been accomplished without the encouragement and patience of our families.

We would also like to thank Dr. James Drylie for his contribution to this project, and GFO Designs for the cover layout.

INTRODUCTION

The history of law enforcement in the United States spans three-and-a-half centuries. In its earliest days, law enforcement amounted essentially to the efforts of citizens who volunteered to provide watchman-type duties in their colonies. Their ventures were not complicated. They left their families, day and night, to take their posts in the community so their families, as well as others' families, would be protected.

As the need for law enforcement increased in America, corollary growth in its nature and scope followed. A general theme is apparent in this growth: Law enforcement developed from simple, uncomplicated functions involving little stress into complex and stressful endeavors requiring highly trained personnel. The complexities imposed, and the concurrent stress these complexities created, impacted the officers as well as their families. Thereafter, the creation and slow evolution of psychological services for law enforcement officers and their families began.

The earliest involvement of behavioral scientists in the law enforcement field appeared to be about 1916 (Vollmer, 1921). However, it had virtually nothing to do with the well-being of police officers or their families. The scientists' activities pertained solely to the selection of police candidates; they were employed part-time to do psychological testing.

Subsequently, the assistance of behavioral scientists expanded from psychometrics to include providing operational help in such matters as hostage negotiation, criminal personality profiling, domestic crisis intervention, crime scene analysis, post-critical-incident care, and general counseling with police officers regarding personal problems and the problems inherent in police work.

These early efforts came together in 1968 when the Los Angeles, California, Police Department hired a full-time police psychologist (Dr. Martin Reiser), thereby giving formal recognition to the importance of behavioral scientists in law enforcement. Some feel that this event marked the birth of police psychology as a specialty field within the field of psychology. Police psychology developed notably thereafter.

This development has been marked by a steady increase in the number of police departments employing full-time and/or part-time psychologists, the growing number of conferences and symposia wherein police psychologists share their successes and failures in law enforcement settings, and the 1982 recognition by the

American Psychological Association of police psychology by designating a special section of an affiliate for psychologists who work in law enforcement. These developments are evidence that psychological services in police organizations in the United States have become an essential component of contemporary law enforcement programs.

The history of the development of psychological services in law enforcement in the United States has as its cornerstone the history of policing. It is through an understanding of the origin of policing, as well as the ever-changing role of the police in society, that a clear understanding can be achieved with regard to the need for psychological services and the eventual implementation of these services in law enforcement. The field of psychological services in law enforcement organizations has continued to develop in spite of the skeptics who have long denounced the need for such services. Psychological services are now an integral part of most police departments' administrations and thus an integral part of the mental health maintenance of police officers throughout the country

cover memo (Reese, 1987).

THE CHANGING ROLE OF THE AMERICAN POLICE OFFICER

The Praetorian Guard of the Roman Emperor Augustus, responding to the problems of urban society and maintaining order, is generally regarded as the precursor of the police function as it is known today throughout the world. Augustus appointed a Praefectus Urbi in 27 BC. This new official was a regular and permanent magistrate, whom Augustus invested with all the powers necessary to maintain peace and order in the city. He had the superintendence of butchers, bankers, guardians, and theaters; and to enable him to exercise his power, he had distributed throughout the city a number of milites stationarii, whom we may compare to a modern police force. He also had jurisdiction in cases between slaves and their masters, between patrons and their freedmen, and over sons who had violated the pietas (respect for authority) toward their parents (Hooker, 1996). Policing has thus been in existence for more than two thousand years.

From that time forward it became apparent that the success or failure of societies is based largely upon the ability of their police to maintain order and uphold the laws. Since the institution of the Praetorian Guard, virtually every nation in the world has developed some form of policing, be it military or civilian. More importantly, the success or failure of societies is directly related to the success or failure of their policing activities.

Long before the American colonies claimed their independence from Great Britain, law enforcement became a stabilizing force in the American way of life. The early settlers of America brought with them English common law principles. In that way, the English influenced the American system of law enforcement from the very beginning of colonization.

Early American settlers made efforts to model their police system after that of Great Britain by establishing "watches." They were so called because it was the function of those performing them to merely watch for trouble and to ensure that peace was maintained. Unlike their British counterparts, however, early American settlers tended to be lawbreakers rather than law abiders. The watches were only marginally effective, and thus, Sir Robert Peel's British model of policing, using unarmed uniformed police and military organization, was never permanently adopted in the United States.

"Watches" sprang up in Boston and New Netherlands (now called New York). Other cities adopted the practice of watches. In 1789 the office of the Attorney General of the United States and the United

States Marshals Service were formed. By 1812 the various watches in America were referred to as police. The Boston, Massachusetts, Police Department is generally considered to be the first formal police department in the United States (Reese, 1987).

In 1908, August Vollmer, a chief of police in California, began the Berkeley Police School, the first formal training for police officers in this country. Over the next few years, other cities set up police academies. In 1935, in an effort to keep officers throughout the country knowledgeable regarding technological changes as well as changes in the laws, the first national training school for police, the Federal Bureau of Investigation National Academy, was established (Reese, 1987).

In the United States, the contemporary law enforcement officer is no longer seen as simply an enforcer of laws who accomplishes his mission by virtue of superior force or power. The police profession was highlighted during the 1960s and 1970s when there was a concentration of public concern over civil unrest, widespread crime and ever-increasing crime rates, antiwar demonstrations, and racial disturbances. The police became the one social institution responsible for restoring order (Reese, 1987). This book is an attempt to assist officers and their families in restoring order in their personal lives.

Read this book. It should be read by officers and their spouses alike. If the shoe fits, wear it. Don't beat yourself up, have a pity party, blame the job, or live in the past. If you are divorced or separated, and believe the job may have been the culprit, realize that it could have never been more than a partial factor. Ensure that it was not caused solely by your behavior and/or attitude. Would a new job have saved your marriage? Or would a new attitude have served you better, regardless of your job? If we find other things, such as our jobs, to blame our failures on, none of our failures will ever be our fault. We will continue to find ourselves in new relationships and will not feel obliged to change. If you always do what you've always done, you'll always be what you've always been. Our remedies to repair family issues should begin in our homes with an honest evaluation of how our behavior affects those we love.

It seems logical to ask, "What makes this book unique from any other book on police families?" First, we both have extensive (possibly unequaled) experience and training in this field. However, we come from very different backgrounds, and, therefore, have different perspectives. Both of us are authors and give presentations throughout the world on topics of law enforcement stress, trauma, and coping. One is a law enforcement officer and the other a law enforcement spouse. What we found as two unrelated practitioners in the areas of police wellness was a need to portray the law enforcement officer's family plight in proper perspective, and expose others to the stress and pressures on the officer, the officer's spouse, and their children.

More importantly, this book offers suggestions for solutions. During our discussions with law enforcement officers and their families, we have learned that without a support system, cops fail. Thus, the theme of this book emerges: Our families are our ultimate backup. Without them, we lose, and America loses.

It takes very special people to make up a law enforcement family. We must help families understand who we are and why we think the way we do. Only then can they support us, help us, and, hopefully, change us.

The chapters that follow will shed light on the issues and provide some solutions. Law enforcement is a wonderful and rewarding profession, employing some of the brightest and most sensitive people in the world. We must examine the job, the changes it creates in officers, and its impact upon families. Only then can we truly "serve and protect," not only the public, but the ones we love, to the best of our abilities.

1

DEFINING LAW ENFORCEMENT FAMILIES

> *FAMILIES ARE USUALLY MADE FROM "SCRATCH"*
>
> *"I had convinced my wife that law enforcement was the greatest job in the world and that I would be working with some of the most talented federal, state, and local law enforcement men and women in America, or so I thought. My first FBI assignment was in 1972 in Albany, New York. I worked for J. Edgar Hoover. It was an otherwise quiet day in 1972 when I heard the FBI radio report that a bank had been robbed. In that the bank was FDIC (federally insured), bank robbery is a federal violation. As a "new" agent I responded eagerly. I jumped into my FBI car (a 1968 two-tone green Rambler), took a magnetic "Kojak" light from the back seat, and put it on my vinyl roof. It was then that I confirmed what I already knew; magnets don't stick to vinyl. It was also then that I learned a most important lesson concerning my career: I should look after myself and my loved ones, rather than believing the FBI would do that for me."*
>
> Special Agent James T. Reese (1972)

When one mentions the "law enforcement family," the term conjures up several images. The predominant image throughout the history of law enforcement has been one of police officers serving each other, much as a family would. The perceived mindset is "one for all and all for one"; loyalty to each other before "outsiders"; professional bonding and secrecy; and staying on the correct side of the "thin blue line." Being a member of the "law enforcement family" also meant cops would back each other up, at times without regard for ethics and/or integrity, if they found "one of their own" in harm's way.

Arguably, police officers will often do anything to protect each other, and just as often the courts may disagree with their choices of action. Other officers are their "family" and, therefore, no price is too great for coming to each other's rescue. Thus all bets are off when any one of these "family members" is at risk.

Unfortunately, the real law enforcement families are at risk. The risks are well-known in law enforcement circles and it is an accepted fact that many law enforcement families are in trouble. Often, the source of that trouble is the spouse who wears the badge. The badge is full of authority and power, but never big enough to hide behind or powerful enough to solve personal problems. It may be called a shield in some jurisdictions, but the size of this shield pales in comparison to the size of the shield they actually need: a shield that will protect them spiritually, emotionally, and physically. (For a look at relevant issues and challenges facing police officers today, see Take Up the Shield, Miano, 2005).

When one outside the "law enforcement circle" is called upon to define a law enforcement officer, we hear descriptive terms such as authoritative, commanding, powerful, ruthless at times, opinionated, judgmental, self-assured (often to the point of arrogance), secretive, and paranoid. Well, guess what? There is a place in law enforcement for all these characteristics and behaviors. What the average person, not intimately knowledgeable of the job of enforcing the law, frequently neglects to note these officers' additional qualities as givers, servants, protectors, people dedicated to helping others, risking their life and limb for people they don't know, leaving their families to help other families. They are compassionate, charitable with their time and talents, and, sadly in many cases, victims of the very system of justice they are sworn to enforce. They give freely, do not ask for sympathy, and serve others daily.

Police officers can and often do become vicarious victims—stressed, altered, and in some cases destroyed by the crimes they investigate (Reese and Horn, 1988). The job of the officer pushes and pulls from many directions, causing the officer to play the hard nut in one situation, and then move smoothly into the role of sympathetic helper in the next. Often he or she will choose to ignore or repress the emotional problems of role conflict, ambiguity, and subsequent stress caused by "shifting gears" between the various roles. The stress of law enforcement can produce family problems, leading to the use of unsystematic and often counterproductive defense mechanisms (e.g., isolation of affect), and, ultimately, burnout.

Law enforcement officers leave their homes every day and battle evil, cruelty, crime, injustice, the courts, their supervisors, the administration, and the system in general. It seems to them that even when they win, they lose. The price they pay for "winning" is exhaustive and, often, not considered worth their efforts. They come home as "walking wounded," looking for solace, peace of mind, a little respect, and some kindness. After their day ends and all the arguments with the public, their superiors, peers, and the courts have ended; the gunfire has subsided; the arrests are made; the raids are conducted—after the "smoke" has virtually settled on their day—they seek peace. These, after all, are peace officers. "Blessed are the peacemakers" (Mathew 5:9). Officers interviewed and/or debriefed by Doctor Reese at the FBI Academy following critical incidents and those attended to by Mrs. Castellano following the tragedy of

September 11, 2001, at the World Trade Center in Manhattan, questioned why they should not be able to personally experience the peace they strive for in society. Some are fortunate enough to come home to the ultimate backup: the law enforcement family. Home should be a place for healing, understanding, peace of mind, love, and compassion. For other officers, however, the family merely becomes another source of stress rather than a respite from it. Sometimes it is because they do not bring any peace, respect, or kindness home with them. They merely expect to find it there.

The physical dangers of being a cop already are vastly overrated by TV and movies, while no one pays attention to the more serious emotional dangers of the job that drive cops to divorce, suicide, and alcohol abuse and other drug addiction. Stress in police work is real, and is dangerous emotionally for both officer and family. Civilians have seldom understood the real danger inherent in police work. It has never been particularly hazardous to the body, not since Sir Robert Peel first organized his corps of bobbies. "This line of work has always been a threat to the spirit" (Wambaugh, 1987).

Contemporary law enforcement officers must function as counselors, social workers, psychologists, negotiators, and investigators, as well as traditional police officers. Their work fluctuates from dull and boring to moments of sheer panic, when life-and-death decisions have to be made in a matter of seconds, and back again. These combinations of factors in police work, dealing with terrible situations and traumatized victims, and working under the threat of physical danger, result in overwhelming stress.

It is this unusual amount of stress (Paton and Violanti, 2006) that makes explicable the belief that police officers in the United States have high rates of problem drinking, suicide (Violanti, 1996), and divorce. "How exactly does stress cause attitude and behavioral changes, impair family and social relationships, and develop cynicism, apathy, and an unwillingness to seek help?" (Reese, Horn and Dunning, 1991). It is caused by denial of relevant issues and need for control.

In the profession of law enforcement, there are few places where officers can feel safe and at ease. Logic would dictate that the primary place for this feeling of ease should be in their homes. Some officers can "retreat" there to mend—but not all. Many law enforcement families experience a form of domestic disturbance unknown in non-law-enforcement families. It is brought home from work and manifests itself in the day-to-day events of one's personal life. Wives turn into single moms due to dad's preoccupation with his work. Police families receive little support and, after a time, learn to live without it.

In homes where the female is the officer, a similar scenario takes place. In many cases, the husband resents the need for him to perform "motherly" functions due to the absence of his law enforcement wife. Additionally, some officers stay at work late because going home is not a pleasant experience (Bartolome, 1983). This is not a new phenomenon or avoidance behavior, nor is it restricted to law enforcement. It is still, however, counterproductive behavior.

Much has been written about the law enforcement occupation. As early as 1976 the stress of being a police officer was extensively researched and stressors were identified. The first full-time police psychologist in America, Dr. Martin Reiser (now retired) of the Los Angeles Police Department, stated that these stressors can have as much an effect on the officer's family as they do on the officer (Reiser, 1972). In 1976, Dr. John Stratton, formerly with the Los Angeles County Sheriff's Office, wrote a book, Police Passages, in which he detailed the difficulties faced by law enforcement families (1984). Doctor Stratton, together with the late Dr. Harold Russell, co-author of a landmark book on police psychology (Russell and Beigel, 1991), Doctor Reiser, Dr. Michael Roberts, the first police psychologist with the San Jose Police Department, and retired FBI Supervisory Special Agent John Minderman are considered by many to be pioneers in the field of police psychology.

All families have plans for achieving certain goals. Some of these plans are formal, while others are not. Families of police officers are no exception. In many instances the law enforcement occupation can upset, alter, or even destroy family plans or strategies for success. The police officer must be considered a part of the whole (more or less a family therapy concept), rather than be considered separately (Reese, 1987).

POLICE STRESS IS UNIQUE—POLICE FAMILIES ARE SPECIAL!

Throughout history, the family life of police personnel has been tremendously affected by the increased occupational demands and stress of their work. This is so much the case that the police family has been empirically referred to as a high-risk lifestyle (Depue, 1981). According to Bibbins (1986), "The stressors of shift work, the constant reality of life-or-death considerations, negativity and apathy from the public, court system requirements, regulations and limitations, isolation and boredom, and organizational practices inherent to police organizations, are some of the central forces which are believed to contribute pressure and strain on police personnel."

As early as 1983, a project was conducted for the National Institute of Mental Health to describe the stresses of emergency and disaster workers (Hartsough and Myers, 1985). Three major sources of stress were observed and identified. They were occupational stress, organizational stress, and traumatic incident stress. The same three sources provide a useful structure for looking at the sources of stress for the spouses of law enforcement officers (Hartsough, 1991).

Scrivner and Reese (1994) suggest that police families, though not part of the organization, are very much affected by it. Over and above the prevailing fear for the safety of their loved ones, members of the police family experience pressures typically not found in other occupations. These pressures occur at all levels. They vary from a new recruit's family learning to manage the presence of a weapon in the home and the fear of being alone on midnight shifts, to those of a police chief's family coping with the personal anguish and public scrutiny that occurs when a chief is embroiled in a community controversy.

In between, a variety of other job-related issues take their toll on family life and contribute to family dysfunction. Some of the more salient issues were highlighted in 1991 testimony before the House Select Committee on Children, Youth, and Families (U.S. House of Representatives, 1991).

Among the culprits causing family disruption, rotating shifts play a dominant role. First of all, shift work disrupts family life for all police families and interferes with holidays and family special events. Also, family plans for scheduled days off are jettisoned when an officer is called for court.

Rotating shifts also create "single law enforcement parents." These are generally women and they are particularly affected by the struggle to provide adequate child care and a family life while supporting a spouse whose rotating shifts are disruptive to a normal family life.

Lastly, over time, shift work can exact a physical toll on the officer. This toll can be manifested in emotional changes such as irritability and increased tension at home or actual physical disabilities.

Shift work is now, and always will be, a law enforcement nemesis. Shift work is not the entire problem by itself. Rather, the operational environment where police shifts occur is unpredictable, crisis-driven, and subject to emergency response. Hence, the overarching message communicated to the members of the police family is that the job takes priority over their needs; the family must wait and see if the law enforcement spouse "has time for them."

The above phenomena occur in an occupation where destabilizing events challenge a family with some frequency. Added to the stress of shift work, a law enforcement family soon learns to live with the fear of death, but quickly learns that the potential for nonfatal physical injury is greater and poses a greater financial threat. Death is usually followed by insurance payments and other offers of assistance. Injuries can force disability retirement upon an officer. Often, this is financially catastrophic. On-the-job injuries have long-term career ramifications that can adversely affect income potential for an officer and the family.

Equally destabilizing is the risk of an officer becoming the target of an internal investigation. Whether the investigation is due to a serious infraction or to a frivolous complaint, an officer's family members bear the burden of events for which they had no responsibility. Consequently, here again they fear financial ruin, as well as the embarrassment and humiliation of social ostracism.

JOB-RELATED PERSONAL CHANGES AND FAMILY RELATIONSHIPS

Injuries and investigations are commonplace in law enforcement and are not just isolated career events. Yet, the more prevailing family concerns appear to be how the job affects a police officer personally, and how observed personal changes influence family relationships. Law enforcement is not just about apprehending criminals. Interwoven into the fabric of work is ongoing contact with the social problems of the community, a contact that often begins to sow the seeds of cynicism.

Seeing more human tragedy in the first three years of a career than most people see in a lifetime, a new officer's idealism is tested and innocence lost. Thus, an officer begins to construct psychological shields as protection against becoming emotionally overwhelmed. The psychological shield does not remain in the locker room. Inevitably, it goes home with the officer, where it is perceived as a lack of sensitivity to family issues. In relationships already strained by the growing suspiciousness, hypervigilance, overprotectiveness, and mistrust of other people that develop with time on the job, this shield creates new barriers.

Police work gradually influences communication styles and problem-solving skills. However, the same styles and skills that work well on the street can be counterproductive at home and contribute to family dysfunction.

A LAW ENFORCEMENT HUSBAND'S VIEW (REESE)

Throughout the twenty-five years when I held the titles of husband and law enforcement officer simultaneously, I had many work-related calls that interrupted my life. I always tried to provide my wife with as much information as possible regarding why I had been called into action. I believed then, and still believe now, that as my spouse she had a right to know; that providing her with enough information to "get her out of the dark" was the considerate thing to do because she was my support system. Please note that my first boss was J. Edgar Hoover, the first Director of the FBI. His unique leadership style seemed to encourage us all to live our lives in secrecy, to put the job first, to distance ourselves from our families in particular and society in general. Many feared him—I merely respected and tolerated him.

Fortunately, I believed early on that I worked for him, but my wife didn't. I believed myself to be an intelligent person who could make some personal decisions about what to share with my family and what not to share. I always tried to provide as much information as I could about the nature of the call so my wife would know about my activities and trust me to do my job and take care of myself. I believed that if I provided too little information, I would create fear and mistrust.

I also limited what I did. I was not the "go-to guy" for our "neighborhood watch." Too often law enforcement officers believe their neighborhood's safety is their responsibility. I never shared that belief. In fact, Ronald Kessler, in one of his New York Times best-selling books entitled *The Bureau*, quotes an exchange Doctor Reese had with a training class for new FBI agents. Kessler writes, " 'When you mow the lawn, you're still the FBI,' James T. Reese would instruct new agents at Quantico. Agents may be asked by neighbors to intervene in situations they should avoid. 'You should tell them to call the police,' Reese told them. "What you do is give them a logical explanation for why we are not Batman" (Kessler, 2002, 234).

During the past thirty-five years, I have been intimately associated with the topic of law enforcement stress. I have heard an untold number of excuses for domestic discord in police families. Some officers say the kind of work they do prohibits them from letting their spouses know too much about their duties. When the phone rings at night, they simply say, "It's work," and leave the house without answering questions or explaining. To say this approach seems to be unfair is an understatement.

I have been assigned to fugitive squads, foreign counterintelligence assignments, undercover operations, and general criminal work. I have worked locally and have flown internationally to do my job. Never did I consider it proper to keep my wife ignorant concerning what I was doing. She has always been my partner in life . . . and my ultimate backup. I believed that if the FBI could trust me with a handgun, they could also trust me with a secret. I certainly know when to shoot and when to talk, and when not to do both!

Even when security matters dictated that she not be privy to everything, I told her what I could. She was always satisfied with that; she trusted me; I never lied to her about my work.

Too often, officers try to build their support system at the very minute they need it. That is too late. A support system must be built so it will be in place when needed. As an example of how a support system works, allow me to provide the following example in my life:

After helping to assist in the psychological decompression of the brave members of New Jersey Task Force One at the World Trade Center shortly after the attack on September 11, 2001, I returned home. I recall my wife asking me, "How are you, honey?" I said, to the best of my recollection, "I'm all right." To this day, I know she knew I wasn't. But again, she's my ultimate backup. She listened, allowed me to have my feelings, whether exposed or hidden, and gave me time to cope in a personal way. Afterward, we talked, airing our emotional feelings regarding the event, and continued with our lives, together. Neither one of us has ever tried to be bigger or braver than the other. That's not how successful teams win.

A husband's attempt to repair family issues should begin at home with an honest personal evaluation of how he believes his behavior and the impact of his job affect those he loves. Sometimes it may be necessary to ask, "How are we doing?" "What do you see changing?" By asking honest questions, you will receive honest answers, which will help you alter your behavior if deemed necessary.

A LAW ENFORCEMENT WIFE'S VIEW (CASTELLANO)

Never in my wildest dreams did I think I would be the wife of a police officer. No one in my family was in law enforcement, not even the military in any significant way. My husband was not in police work when we met, but the desire to serve as an officer was always in the back of his mind. I was providing counseling services and coordination for a project in Newark when suddenly I noticed the police officers in that city were being victimized. Everyone was arranging care for the criminals and the victims of the crimes, but nothing was being done to assist the psychological needs of the police officers themselves.

Subsequently I started to provide treatment for police officers and before long I was moved to create programs to assist them. As I was pulled into the world of police psychology my husband decided he would join the ranks of law enforcement. I remember that when he got the letter of acceptance from the Prosecutor's Office, and we knew he was on his way to the academy, we were thrilled.

Just as he was leaving to go to the academy we had our first child, and his departure for six months was an emotional one. This was the first time I realized I was going to have to get used to being alone as a police wife. My husband received the merit award at his police academy graduation and although the six months home alone with our baby was trying, that moment in time stood still as one of the proudest moments of my life. My husband is my hero. Too often police traits are viewed negatively, when in fact, in their purest form, they can be positive assets as well. The traits I see in him as a law enforcement officer are the very same traits that ensure success in our family.

As Reese Witherspoon quoted June Carter's favorite phrase at the 2007 Academy Awards, "I'm just trying to matter." As the "ultimate backup," "I'm just trying to matter" to the people I am blessed to love, my husband and our children, regardless of his call to duty. I am committed to view this world as a police wife. And it's a view I intend to enjoy with pride and adoration until the day I die. My children and I are honored to be my husband's ultimate backup every day of our lives.

As we define our own police families we recognize that each family unit is unique in many ways. Why is it difficult to define a police family? Police families differ in makeup as much as any other families. Thus, there is no stereotypical "police family" any more than there is a stereotypical "cop." There are no books or analyses about bankers' families or lawyers' families. The law enforcement family is examined here because the police culture is so unique and encompassing, our families remain an integral part of this culture.

2

THE LAW ENFORCEMENT ENCULTURATION PROCESS AND FAMILY LIFE CYCLE

"FITTING IN AT WORK" CAN RESULT IN BEING
"LEFT OUT AT HOME"

Early in my FBI career, I would learn that working cases with the FBI, together with state and local law enforcement, usually involved stopping on the way home for a beer at the end of the day. I was new to the area, and to the FBI. I continually chose not to join them. I chose instead to go home, to be with my new bride. The others continued to go to the bars. I had no objection to what they chose to do.

There were a few who disliked me for failing to take part in their "choir practice" following work. I was approached by one agent who indicated that my lack of desire to join them for a drink reflected a lack of commitment to the office and left them with the impression that I did not like the people I worked with. I assured them that my not spending part of the night with them had nothing to do with whether or not I liked them. Rather, it had to do with my wanting to go home at the end of the day to spend time with my best friend, my wife. I understand that some of the agents may not have had such an option.

I chose to exercise my rights to live by my rules, not theirs. It always takes a certain amount of courage to be different. I had made a commitment to my wife. I am pleased to say that I continued to go home to my wife and daughter during my FBI career, and I still do.

Approximately three months after this incident, one of the individuals who had confronted me regarding my not drinking with them approached me and said, "Thanks." I asked him what he was thanking me for. He replied, "No one stops for drinks anymore." I told him that was their choice and that all I was doing was that which I was committed to do. He interrupted that it was my example that led the others to quit the habit of stopping each night. He said that my behavior made the others stop and think. More importantly, he said that his son approached him the night before and told him, "Gee, Dad, you don't smell like beer all the time anymore."

Special Agent James T. Reese (1973)

Dr. Martin Reiser was the first to identify the changes that occur in officers during their career. He contends there is an enculturation process in police work that shapes young officers. This shaping can take place as early as their initial training at the police academy (Reiser, 1972).

It is true that attitude is often the first thing people notice about you. We all change in the course of our lives. Some change is for the better, some is not.

Usually, the person changing is in the worst position to judge the quality of that change. The people around them, however, particularly those who live with them, have a front row seat.

Consider the fact that police recruits learn more than just skills for policing. They learn about the "police image" from the examples and attitudes of veteran law enforcement officers. The image portrayed is not always positive and can be counterproductive. The first notable personality change identified by psychologists in young officers has been termed the "John Wayne Syndrome" (Reiser, 1986).

This is a grouping of behaviors that reflect "macho" thinking and a loss of sensitivity for the public they serve. They become very authoritarian, always in command, unwilling to lose, never admitting to mistakes, paranoid, unforgiving, and distrustful of others. This behavior serves as a form of self-preservation and emotional control. Its impact on the police family is significant and must be recognized and addressed.

Law enforcement families generally have everyday challenges and solutions. When officers are authoritative, in command, suspicious, cynical, hypervigilant, and action-oriented, it affects their families. Families are affected dramatically as they often take on the officer's characteristics. These families separate themselves from society, choose friends carefully, expect model behavior from their children, and are slaves to the job.

The enculturation process occurs in parallel phases for both the officer and his family. Despite the unique assignments and diversity in agencies, the life cycle of a law enforcement officer's career remains an almost universally common experience (Kirschman, 1997). The following headings will show the various phases of enculturation: for each phase, one view of how the officer is affected, and a parallel view of the family.

POLICE OFFICER / PHASE ONE

We initially identify officers' experiences during the applicant phase. Like most applicants, they have no idea what they are getting into. The application process is generally accepted to be arduous and lengthy. It involves written exams, physical exams, interviews, and more. The pressures from the hiring department are spelled out. Family stressors are "off the charts" with no help in sight. The questions from spouses are endless. Family members want to know what the job entails. Will it be a dangerous job? Little do they know that most of the stresses of law enforcement are kept within the "thin blue line" of secrecy.

People apply for the position for a myriad of reasons. Most applicants really believe they can make a difference. Most veterans aren't sure they have made as much as a dent in crime, not to mention a difference. New recruits and their families, however, continue on the path, hoping this new career will be a path to success.

POLICE FAMILY / PHASE ONE

During this phase police families are hopeful, with limited trepidation about their spouse/parent's opportunity to work in the field of law enforcement. Unless they are from a police family most will draw upon their limited knowledge of the law enforcement lifestyle based on TV and the media. Police families, particularly spouses, may be hopeful their loved one will be accepted into the law enforcement culture.

Along with a variety of background checks and ethical questions, a self-inventory for the applicant occurs during this phase. Family members may also do a family inventory, feeling pressure to support their loved one. Leading the lifestyle of a law enforcement family implies all involved will behave as "model" citizens.

There are many variables in the applicant phase that contribute to an officer being selected, and inevitably some anxiety and doubt occurs in anticipation of the final outcome. Overall the police family as a unit remains hopeful and enthusiastic for the opportunity to serve together and for the chance to perform the duties of public servants in their community.

POLICE OFFICER / PHASE TWO

The enculturation process begins "formally" in the police academy phase of an officer's career. In early police literature, this transformation of the normal personality of recruits into the police personality was attributed to an "enculturation process" (Reiser, 1972). Applicants dress alike, speak alike, begin to adapt each other's habits and values, and create some new habits of their own that are mirrored by others. Families are virtually abandoned for months at a time so the applicant can learn a new trade. There is little time to talk, and even less time to be together. The academics are complex; learning the law is intricate, academy discipline strict, and physical requirements grueling. The positive outcome in this phase of the police officer life cycle is that an officer is accepted to the job and is able to successfully complete the intensive training of the police academy.

POLICE FAMILY / PHASE TWO

Sacrifices made by police families begin the first day of the police academy. Most academies require that officers reside away from home, generally for as long as six months, and have limited access to their spouses and children during this time period. As a result police wives and children immediately become enculturated to the notion that the job comes first. The lawn needs to be mowed, garbage must go out, children must be driven to school, a wedding anniversary occurs, and the police spouse and children recognize that their officer in the academy is inaccessible to them.

Police families are motivated by both their love and pride when adapting to being alone while their beloved recruit is away during the academy phase. In addition, if a police officer becomes distracted by activities at home or a family crisis, he or she may not successfully complete the academy. This will impede the success and ultimately the lifestyle of the police family. This phase presents the first glimpse at possible financial hardships, should the officer fail. The academy is the first time spouse and children accept and identify that being alone is a normal part of the police family life cycle.

In a police academy graduation, if one would scan the audience, tears of pride, joy, and sacrifice can be found reflected in the faces of those supporting the new officers. Police academy graduations, especially for those officers who have established successful family units, may be a highlight in the police officers' life cycle. What happens following this phase is critical.

POLICE OFFICER / PHASE THREE

The honeymoon phase can be described as the time period after an officer is sworn in. You are doing the work and bringing home more than just a badge and great stories. Police officers in the family are seen as making a difference in their communities and country. An officer feels a lot of pride pertaining to his duties. A sense of purpose, service, and change sparks an officer's career in this phase. Going to work is actually exciting and meaningful as an officer functions as a public servant.

POLICE FAMILY / PHASE THREE

Police families seem to thrive during this phase. They realize they have great medical benefits and believe they serve as community role models. Respect for the profession, almost a patriotic commitment, occurs within many police families. The officer is happy, as is the family, celebrating public service. All the sacrifices made during the academy phase seem to have paid off for police families now.

POLICE OFFICER / PHASE FOUR

In settling down there is an adaptation to one's routines in terms of shift work and lifestyle changes extremely enmeshed within the police family system. Everyone else comes first. Time for criminals, supervisors, and peers. No time for the family. The hustle and bustle of competitive activity on the job may prompt an officer to be enticed into 'workaholism' should the officer want a promotion.

POLICE FAMILY / PHASE FOUR

In settling down, the police families adapt their routines, balancing shift work and lifestyle changes that may appear the "norm." Eating, relaxing, and planning events all reflect a mastering of the science of adaptation to the job for police families. Surrender to the trials and tribulations of the job are also evident for police families as they "settle." Routines can be experienced as comfortable and predictable or resented as monotonous and draining by police family members at this time.

POLICE OFFICER / PHASE FIVE

The disillusionment in the next part of the career has to do with work that seems trite and lacks meaning for an officer. The challenges once cherished on the job seem contaminated by politics or seem impossible in this phase. Many officers will tell you this is where people really begin to figure out if the job is victimizing them and/or if it is something they want to continue.

POLICE FAMILY / PHASE FIVE

Police families try to subvert these changes by offering support, encouragement, and challenges for the officer to combat the disillusionment. Unfortunately, cynicism can be contagious and police families may both agree with and encourage the officer's disillusionment process as they are frustrated as "vicarious victims." Police families begin to decide if the job is victimizing both officer and spouse. This disillusionment has a negative impact on the officer's marriage and family. Spouses may join their officer in a negative spiral due to a "midlife crisis" or financial hardships. Throughout one's career, an officer may feel torn between the police family at work and the police family at home. Hopefully the police family at home is elevated as the priority in this phase.

POLICE OFFICER / PHASE SIX

Coming to a crossroads can reflect professional paranoia; threshold diagnosis; responsibility absorption behavior; and various other forms of compassion fatigue. One soon learns that the ability to serve the public, to support fellow officers, to stay physically healthy and mentally alert, and to create or maintain successful and satisfying interpersonal relationships is dependent largely upon the officer's ability to manage police stress. (See chapter 1 of Into the Minds of

Madmen, Denevi, and Campbell (2004), for specific stress-related issues regarding the effects on author Reese of profiling crime scenes.)

Unfortunately, the subject of stress management wasn't taught at the police academy. Candidates learn that police stress is completely different from the stress of other professions: stress brought on by powers to arrest, search, seize, detain, to use deadly force. Much of the stress of police work is unavoidable; it is brought home each day, albeit silently. Officer candidates are rarely taught how to cope with stress during their academy classes.

POLICE FAMILY / PHASE SIX

For a police family, coming to a crossroads includes asking the question, "Are we going to make it through the tension?" In terms of promotions and going up, going down, or going out, police families teeter with mixed emotions, hoping for a simpler lifestyle yet fearing the change. Resignation, or "settling," offers a way to cope with anxiety and fear for police families. They may also feel the impact of chronic stress and cynicism on each family member.

POLICE OFFICER / PHASE SEVEN

For an officer this phase represents the light at the end

of the tunnel. The sooner you know when you are going to retire, the longer the wait! Anxiety over acclimating to the civilian world may arise. Your future finances and activities also become relative unknowns. Any of the prestige or entitlement accrued in being in law enforcement disappears. Officer isolation and suicide are risks in this phase (Violanti, Castellano, O'Rourke, and Paton, 2006).

POLICE FAMILY / PHASE SEVEN

Retirement for police families re-creates the entire police family life cycle by fostering hope and changes even in those families whose officer has not had a satisfying career. Adjustments to each other and gaps in intimacy may become glaringly obvious during this time.

Most officers retire to other careers, which often are time-consuming and continue to impact their families. Spouses expect retirement to bring their loved ones home. Disappointment and discord may be the result of these unrealized expectations, as, instead of going home, officers go to new and demanding jobs. Ambivalence over a second career is caused by the need for continued income, together with the need for recaptured lost time and intimacy. True partners will dialogue and explore this life crisis together in their best interest.

It is important to recognize that police family building is a "two-way street," and the effort needed to make it work must be equally shared. Wives and children feel, fear, and understand more than police officers realize. Sacrifices are made every day by every member of a police family.

Establishing some rules in life and putting family first seem to always pay off. Perhaps courage will reunite you with your family and serve as an example to inspire others. Some will never follow your example. Some will simply choose to be unhappy and blame the job, their family, and anything else that takes the blame away from themselves.

3

RECAPTURING INTIMACY— REAL PARTNERS

"DO YOU MIND IF I SEARCH YOU?"

PAGING "I LOVE YOU"

During the tragedy of September 11, 2001, I often had to shut off my cell phone to confidentially speak to officers in crisis at Ground Zero. In addition, my husband's duties as a police officer caused his cell phone to be off. Our communication was limited to pagers. During this time we commented to each other that we missed connecting during the day. Because of our duties we were ships passing in the night. We knew it was important to communicate during these trying times. A beautiful ritual emerged. We would page each other and enter the date of our wedding anniversary. The page signified "I love you and I am thinking of you."

Our "I love you" pages seemed to arrive when needed the most. We did the page regularly for two years. When we spoke about it later we were amazed it came just at a moment when I needed to hear it, he told me the same, and it was a very important communication tool for us. It did not take a tremendous effort but had a tremendous impact. Another perk is that we never forget our wedding anniversary! Try it for yourself and regain your romance with your love.

Cherie Castellano, police wife (2001)

Communication is paramount to a law enforcement marriage and family. One must recognize that if an officer's partner or colleague at work knows more about his or her life than the wife or husband, there is acommunication problem. Start talking at home, be creative, and realize that one cannot not communicate. Only by communicating can you maintain intimacy in your life.

EXPECTATIONS AND DEMANDS IN THE PARTNERSHIP

Most police mental health professionals agree that a career in law enforcement can represent a significant intrusion into family life. This phenomenon was defined in a classic study (Niederhoffer and Niederhoffer, 1978) as "job responsibilities superseding family relationships." According to the study and in light of their observations about the pernicious and powerful influence police work can have on police officers' spouses and families, it is apt that Niederhoffer and Niederhoffer (1977) should have nominated police work as a "jealous mistress" (Alexander, 1994). Another striking finding by Maynard and Maynard (1982) was that about three quarters of police officers' wives believed that their husbands regarded their police work as more important to them than their own families.

What are some of the expectations?

Communities frequently hold officers and their families to a different standard of behavior in comparison with individuals in other occupations. Not only do community members expect officers to be readily available in off hours to respond to neighborhood infractions, they expect law enforcement families to be free from family conflicts and to unhesitatingly respond positively each time the officer is called to duty.

Children are also expected to behave differently when their parent is a police officer. Such expectations can be particularly troublesome for police officers' adolescent children if they are held to different behavior standards than their peers. Their parent is different from other kids'.

Nowhere is this intrusion into family life more apparent than in the requirement in most jurisdictions for officers to carry their weapons on a 24-hours basis, and, when needed, to take appropriate police action. Thus, a pleasant family outing can quickly be disrupted by police work that turns into an unpleasant police event. It is not unusual for police family members to experience loneliness and alienation and to develop resentment for the pervasive influence that a career in law enforcement assumes over their lives.

Under the Shadow of the Badge

As there are some definable officer traits and stressors, there are comparable experiences and stresses identified with police families. Police work continually calls upon the resources of all family members. A wife will resent the term "pig" and defend her husband and his profession in the face of all odds. The daughter worries about returning home late from a date because she knows "the cop" will be waiting to interrogate her and/or her friends. The teenage son's friends dare him to drink because "his Dad's a cop." He may drink just to prove a point to his friends that he is just like them.

A total focus on one's job places everything else in your life on the "back burner." Yes, there are times when total focus may be the difference between life and death. There also appears to be an obligation, if not a duty, to refocus following a day's work. We must acknowledge that we work in an imperfect system and that each of us lives a somewhat imperfect life. We must have flexibility in our dealings with family and understand they, too, are imperfect.

The law enforcement family is so dear to our hearts, and yet so foreign to all we have been taught. Families are those support systems that assist us in achieving goals. How is the law enforcement family different from any other family? To begin with they tend to live "under the shadow of the badge." The responsibility the officer has looms over them every minute of every day. It commands attention, consumes time, and can even take his or her life. Law enforcement spouses cannot tell their officers to pay less attention to the job. That may lead them into harm's way. Therefore, spouses ask officers to be more cognizant of issues at home when they are there. Soon, the officer spends less time there so as to not have to deal with the "mundane" family issues. This is merely a defense mechanism.

The process by which defense mechanisms are developed hinges on the individual's perception. For an event to be stressful, it must be perceived as such in the mind. How one perceives a situation will largely dictate one's response. The defense known as isolation of affect, for example, allows the emotional part of an issue to be "set aside."

Defense mechanisms may be thought of as mental functions that protect an individual from internal and/or external threats, conflicts, impulses, and hurts. Those significant in police work include, among others, isolation of affect, displacement, substitution, repression, rationalization, and projection. Defense mechanisms were first identified by Sigmund Freud in

1894 in his study The Neuro-psychoses of Defence. Anna Freud (1936) identified these defenses by name; H.P. Laughlin (1979) differentiated among twenty-two major defenses, twenty-six minor defenses, and three special reactions and combinations. Of these, several have been identified by police psychologists as being used frequently by law enforcement officers.

It would appear, due to an overuse of defense mechanisms, law enforcement officers often become vicarious victims: changed, altered, and sometimes destroyed by the crimes they investigate. The job pushes and pulls in many directions. In a paradoxical way, the job demands one play the hard nut in some situations and then move flawlessly into the position of a helping role. While self-deception can have positive values, in this case deceiving oneself about the emotional concerns of role conflict, and the emotional stress and strain caused by shifting gears into the various roles, can be counterproductive.

The stress of law enforcement can produce family problems, leading to the use of these unsystematic and often counterproductive defense mechanisms—, for example, isolating emotions. Thus, family members should be educated to identify the early warning signs of maladaptation to police stress. This is important in that family members are in the best position to see the changes that occur in their law enforcement spouse/parent, and can draw appropriate attention to it in a timely and kind fashion.

Perhaps one of the most deceptive, and, if not controlled, emotionally dangerous defenses used by officers is that of isolation of affect. *Isolation of affect* (otherwise known as isolation of emotion) is in use when an altered perception of reality (i.e., the ability to view events less intensely) permits the officer to appear in control at all times. This provides an officer the ability to live up to his "take charge" image, and to deny any emotional stake in the situation.

Unfortunately, while this defense may serve the officer well at the scene of a fatal automobile accident or similar traumatic event, it is difficult to turn emotions on and off at will. Thus, this need to bury emotions continues into one's private life. Soon, spouses and other family members are living with officers who are emotionally withdrawn, unable to express themselves, and unable to see that the defense that works so well on the job is destroying meaningful interpersonal relationships, reducing intimacy, and cheating them of their feelings.

"Image armor," the need for an officer to be protected from his or her emotions, plays an enormous role in the destruction of interpersonal relationships. If nothing else separates us from other animals, emotions do. Human beings' emotions are an essential component of their very existence. Without emotions, we are not much unlike all other animals: merely seeking food and shelter, and needing to reproduce our kind.

Unfortunately, law enforcement officers begin to isolate their emotions as early as the police academy. They learn this isolation from watching veteran officers talk with apparent emotional detachment about horrible events. They soon experience on a personal level how emotions can interfere with their ability to perform their duties. Emotions then become a liability.

Initially they fight for control of their emotions. Later they learn to simply not allow emotions to show. They isolate them so they can better perform their duties. Turning them off seems to be quite easy; turning them back on, however, is difficult for many.

Displacement is in operation when an emotional feeling is transferred, deflected, and redirected from its internal object to a substitute external one. This is often as simple as chopping wood to release hostility.

Regression has been referred to as the primary and most important ego defense. It is the automatic, effortless, and involuntary assignment or relegation of consciously repugnant or intolerable ideas, impulses, and feelings to the unconscious. An example may be a rape victim who knows her assailant but has no conscious memory of him.

Rationalization is used when the ego justifies or attempts to modify otherwise unacceptable impulses, needs, feelings, behavior, and motives into ones that are consciously tolerable and acceptable. It is the most frequently used mechanism. Officers rationalize why they became officers, why they work sex crimes, why rapes occur, and why they have become the type of person they are.

Finally, projection is a defense of major importance. Known as the defense of "blaming others," projection occurs when consciously disowned aspects of self are rejected or disowned and thrown outward, to become imputed to others. Often, people ascribe to others characteristics they detest in themselves.

There are many more defenses. Defense mechanisms are used daily and productively by all people—so it's all right if readers have identified some of these defenses in their lives. But these defenses can become counterproductive if they are habitually used to excess, for the wrong reasons, or in the wrong place.

Humor: The serious side of policing

An adjunct to emotional isolation is grotesque humor, the kind that is not funny and is not meant to be. "Sick" humor works. It helps to maintain an officer's sanity because it acts as a safety valve and lessens the emotional impact of the crime or situation. Unlike burying emotions within you, in this case the officer, in effect, reaches out to others instead of sitting on his emotions.

By speaking the unspeakable and being understood, he can ventilate his wounded feelings and share his pain. It allows the "venom" to escape from his thoughts and prevents him from emotionally poisoning himself. Among other uses, humor has been said to reduce anger, vengeance, and feelings of helplessness.

Using such humor as a release, however, is usually very controlled. It is expressed only within earshot of fellow law enforcement officers who are directly involved, and, conventionally, only veterans can get away with it. It is almost as if they have "paid their emotional dues" and thus have earned the privilege to use such humor without being chastised. It is as if they have no more emotions to invest and have all but used up their coping mechanisms.

As long as sick humor is closely monitored by its practitioners, it performs a useful function. Once it finds its way out of the locker room or crime scene and into the public eye, it is a clear sign of maladaptation to the stress encountered. An example: After pulling out of a river, a drowned organized crime member wrapped in chains, a veteran detective utters, "worst suicide I've ever seen." Other detectives may grin, and perhaps the immediate shock and gruesomeness of the horrible homicide subsides. Because of the remark, they are able to get on with the unspeakable part of their jobs.

Remember, this humor is not meant to be funny, just therapeutic. If outsiders such as the press were to hear it, these officers would be labeled as sick, callous, and mentally morbid. After years and years of such gruesome discoveries, even the humor becomes unnecessary. They simply do their jobs emotionless and go home like zombies. They lose their emotions, lose the joy in their lives, and fail to see all that their families can provide them to improve their mental health.

This type of humor must be differentiated from cynicism. Usually, cynicism comes from the lower levels of law enforcement challenging the decisions of the hierarchy; doing more with less; and the ungrateful public.

Anger

Anger damages intimate relationships. Anger creates

emotional scar tissue just like cutting your skin forms scars. An age-old cliché states, "Anger is the poison we swallow hoping the other guy will die."

David and Vera Mace, pioneers in the Marriage Enrichment movement, have outlined a way of coping with anger feelings that surface in most every marriage relationship. The Maces indicate that anger is a healthy, normal emotion and one that is present at different times in all marital relationships. Couples should give each other the right to be angry. The Maces have developed an acronym to help couples remember a better way of solving anger. The acronym they have selected is AREA. The A stands for Admitting your anger to your spouse; R for Restraining your anger and not letting it get out of hand by blaming or belittling your spouse; E for Explaining in a very calm fashion why you are angry; and A for Action, planning or doing something about the cause of the anger" (http://extension.usu.edu/files/fampubs/anger.htm).

There are those who feel that the expression of anger serves to create healthier and happier communication. Freud's "hydraulic model" believed that energy could get blocked and soon the "lid would fly off" if one did not expel the pressure by being angry. Thus the anger was a catharsis. There are those who believe this is not an acceptable statement today. On the basis of research, Dr. Carol Tavris says, "Today the hydraulic model of energy [used by Freud and others] has been scientifically discredited" (Tavris, 1982, 37).

Anger has its place but may be the most dangerous foe we face. Nancy Missler believes, like Freud, that what is in the unconscious will come out in one way or another. Whether you are aware of the "buried" issues or not, they will begin to motivate your actions. Missler relates that the "justifiable" hurts would cause her to act in an opposite way. Even though her intentions were to act in one way, the unconscious issues were causing her to act in an opposite way. In her attempt to support these notions, Missler uses Romans 7:15, which states, "For that which I do I allow not: for what I would, that do I not; but what I hate, that do I" (http://www.psychoheresy-aware.org/nmissler.html).

How are we to avoid and/or control anger? Here are some suggestions: First, we should avoid judgmental terms when discussing a topic that creates anger or when trying to dissipate anger. Try to avoid labeling people in unsavory categories. If something was done or said once, don't play it up as if it is a global and constant issue. Be careful not to send messages of blame and accusation. Let things that have happened in the past remain in the past, thus avoiding history. Life should have a rearview mirror. It is acceptable to glance at the past, to learn from mistakes. However, if one continues to look at the past, sight of the future is lost. Don't make negative comparisons. Keep your body language nonconfrontational, resist making threats, and never attack with your feelings.

Communication is essential when dealing with anger. Be sure to use whole, clear messages. Speak clearly, distinctly, and with focus. Conflict is inevitable, can result in anger, and must be solved by officer and spouse as partners. Due to different needs and opinions, it's OK to have conflicts. It is essential, however, to resolve them. The deterioration that occurs in an officer's idealism can be paralleled to hardening of the heart and decrease in intimacy. Avoid letting the job take away your sense of service or reduce your intimacy with your loved ones. Both are what make you who you are.

Sheri and Bob Stritof (2007) profess that there are some things to never do when you are angry. Among them are never calling one another hurtful names and being sarcastic. Avoid blaming the other person, and if you criticize, ensure that you use criticism to make a point. Walking out of a situation solves nothing, nor does lecturing. Lastly, getting physical is never appropriate.

AN EXAMPLE OF "REAL PARTNERS"

It was August 1979. Our daughter (author Reese) was two-and-a-half years of age. My wife and I had planned to go shopping one night to get some things for my daughter's room.

I recall my wife was on one knee in our living room, putting a little sweater on our daughter when the phone rang. It was shortly after dinner. I answered the phone and can only remember saying, "Yes, sir. Yes, sir. I'll get there as soon as I can, sir." Looking back, an option would have been to not answer the phone. That thought never occurred to me, and I can state that, in my twenty-five-year career, I never failed to answer the phone. I took an oath to be available; I believed it to be the right thing to do.

The call was from my unit chief, the boss of the FBI's Behavioral Science Unit at Quantico, Virginia. As a supervisory special agent of the FBI, I was employed there as an instructor in criminal psychology and criminology, and served as a criminal personality profiler. He informed me there was a plane on the ground at Seattle-Tacoma International Airport with a hijacker on board. The information we had at that time was that a lone male held fifty-five passengers hostage and was demanding a jet, a parachute, and one hundred thousand dollars. The hostage taker had announced he had a bomb in his briefcase.

It was now my duty to tell my wife I could no longer take them shopping. I had to go to work. My wife was disappointed. I would have been disappointed if she wasn't. She asked me why I couldn't go; why did I have to go to work? I told her the circumstances that I had been told, and added that the FBI believed having three profilers in the command center at headquarters in Washington, DC, listening to the negotiations and providing suggestions, might assist in saving the lives of the hostages. Without hesitation she said, "It sounds like they need you more than we do right now. Go ahead, I'll get busy doing something else with Jamie. I know you'll do well. We can go shopping another night."

The personal rule of going home at night when you can makes it less painful to leave at night when you must. Otherwise it's just another night you're not home. Intimacy is exemplified by sacrifice. Police couples sacrifice time with each other for the common good. You cannot love someone without giving of yourself. When you love someone enough to let them go, anticipating the joy their return makes it all worthwhile.

4

MARRIAGE MAINTENANCE

MOVING FROM "ONCE UPON A TIME" TO
"HAPPILY EVER AFTER"

*Early on in my husband's career his job assignments were
fascinating and he would enthusiastically talk to me about a job
only after it was over. Much of his work was undercover, leaving
me never knowing where he was or what he was doing until it was
"public knowledge." My friends often inquired if I worried all the
time that he would get hurt. The answer was always definitively
"no." It was the truth. My confidence in my husband's skills and
ability to defend himself gave me a sense of security. Perhaps it
was denial, but it worked early on. My husband purchased a gun
safe and I felt better about our children not being able to get to his
weapons by accident. I worried more about the gun in our house
than I did about my husband in the city streets doing drug raids.
Many wives have told me they hate having guns in their homes.
They also realize it is a primary tool of their spouse's trade and its
presence is not negotiable.*

*Overtime and long hours started my "independent woman" police
wife mentality. Too many events, dates, holidays, and tickets to a
show went awry because my husband got stuck at work. Crime is
not a "nine-to-five" activity. Eventually I figured out being
independent meant always having a "Plan B" to support my
husband's career. If not I would have tortured him with*

resentment and nagging for all of the missed moments. I chose to cherish the time with him and adapt my plans. Often I was sad rather than mad because I missed him.

The transformation into an "independent police wife" has largely been a positive experience in my life. I believe in what my husband does. His job has caused me to become more independent. This independence has served me and our marriage well and I consider it an asset. My sacrifices would be in vain for material gain. When my husband goes to work he is trying to be the best public servant he can be. When I burn the London broil or wait up until two a.m. until he comes in the door, I am serving the public by supporting him. My sacrifices are not in vain or just to stay happily married. I am his partner in life, and in that role I get to be part of his public service through my support. My commitment as a law enforcement spouse confirms my convictions and willingness to maintain my marriage.

Cherie Castellano (2007)

Marriage is an age-old institution. While there are many opinions concerning the character and makeup of a marriage, it is universally considered the dedication of two persons to each other. Marriage supposedly ushers in an era in the lives of the married couple of selflessness, humility, patience, and love. Humility ushers in the concept of being humble. Some believe that by being humble, you "think less of yourself." In actuality, being humble really means that you "think of yourself less!" The vows of marriage historically include language that calls for two persons who are to be married to agree to say together these vows: "to have and to hold from this day forward; for better, for worse, for richer, for poorer, in sickness and in health, to love and to cherish, till death us do part"; or to answer this question: "Wilt thou have this woman (man) to thy wedded wife (husband), to live together according to God's law in the holy estate of Matrimony? Wilt thou love her, comfort her, honour and keep her, in sickness and in health? and, forsaking all other, keep thee only unto her, so long as ye both shall live?" (The Registrars of the Convocations of Canterbury and York, 1965, 1966).

Today, as in the past, courtships, whether long or short in duration, fail to explore all the variables in a relationship. The courtship fails to examine the possibilities of success in a relationship prior to embarking on this lifelong journey of togetherness. Courtships are often short, meaning the two know little about each other's likes and dislikes, much less understanding and recognizing their numerous moods and needs. Statistics make one wonder if knowing someone better, in fact, raises the probability that couple will stay together. Some family and marriage therapists believe living together for years prior to a marriage does not decrease the chances of a divorce, and may even increase them!

Courtships are often short and marriages spontaneous. Individuals can meet over the Internet and at various support groups for single people. Often, there is no time to get to know each other before the question is asked, "Will you marry me?" Due to the speed at which our lives are traveling, the desire to have children while we are young, and the fear of growing old alone, the answer to a proposal of marriage, more often than not, is "yes."

There is no fully rational way, on the basis of a year or so of knowing someone, to predict the next fifty years with that person, and yet this is exactly what the American courtship system demands. Romanticism has been measured by the importance of physical attraction, husband-wife companionship, equality of partners in marriage, and feelings of affection and trust between husband and wife.

Law enforcement can test this relationship like no other. The work of law enforcement can be exciting at one moment and boring the next. Cops live in expectation of what might happen. When excitement does happen, the adrenaline rush, during and following their response, is their reward. It's a reward they are unable to get at home, regardless of what they do. Sooner or later, law enforcement officers seem to become addicted to the "rush" of police work.

The law enforcement officer/spouse/parent is often silent (when not silent, opinionated) and resistant to being wrong; is rarely a team player at home; denies being a vicarious victim; discounts the negative impact of trauma experienced as just being "part of the job"; is sometimes viewed by his children as a "know-it-all"; discounts the judgments of others; trusts no one; has few friends (even fewer nonpolice friends); and, has unreasonable expectations for his or her children.

Law enforcement officers may hear from their families: "You're different." "You've changed." "You've become cold, callous, indifferent, almost unfeeling." "Whatever happened to the kind, considerate, gentle, God-fearing, patient, and understanding person I used to know?" Veteran officers have almost certainly heard comments similar to these at some point in their career.

After presenting stress management classes to more than seventy classes (approximately 20,000 officers) at the FBI National Academy and addressing tens of thousands more worldwide throughout the past thirty-five years, I (Reese) can state unequivocally that these comments are common. This is because the officers' profession affects the way they live, impacts upon their willingness, and eventually their ability, to express emotions, and, consequently, affects their interpersonal relationships. The defense mechanism called "isolation of affect" comes into play here (Freud, 1894).

Anything that is expected to work smoothly over a long period of time, or under extreme pressure, must be maintained. An automobile comes with a manual; a water heater comes with a warranty; other products are acquired with guarantees. Your marriage has no manual, warranty, guarantee, or any other protection or outside influence to keep it solid. There is no manual for caring for a spouse, but there are some important components and responsibilities that allow the relationship to succeed. Marriage maintenance must contain, among other things, love, loyalty, honesty, trustworthiness, respect, consideration, humility, caring, giving, listening, sharing, kindness, togetherness, and trust. Knowing that it is impossible to maintain a marriage without having one of these aspects break down, we must add the most important ingredient for maintaining a marriage, forgiveness.

There is very little room for disagreement among commanders when working in a paramilitary setting.

Orders are followed exactly, and very seldom is there any discussion concerning the reasoning for decisions. Consequently, law enforcement officers develop a limited capacity for expressing their feelings. The mentality exemplified by the following comments finds its way into the family setting:

- "Do as I say."
- "Do not question me."
- "I know what is best for this family."
- "I will judge your friends."
- "I am in command."
- "I am the authority."
- "I do not make mistakes."
- "I will not weaken and show emotions."
- "I cannot be hurt."
- "I am never wrong nor am I ever afraid."
- "I do not need any help."

These are obvious attempts to regulate one's life and to pretend to have total control of it. Those officers who begin most sentences with the word I, and pretend to run their lives without any assistance from spouses or other family members, are in peril, as well as denial. Each of us needs a support system of some kind. When we try to r-u-n our life alone, we usually r-u-i-n it. It makes perfect sense—when you put the word "I" in the word run, it spells RUIN! This is a thought worthy of our regard because, eventually, there can be total disengagement from the family.

Satisfaction outside the family and/or marriage is sought due to an apparent impossibility of finding it inside oneself. The distance becomes measurable between officer and spouse, officer and children, or both. It is often measured by the lack of intimacy, the perceived distance each has from the other.

Law enforcement officers must be able to understand and accept the following concepts when it comes to their families:

- They don't have to like your job as much as you do.
- They don't have to behave like law enforcement officers.
- They don't have to talk like cops, or learn the "10-codes."
- They are allowed to have their own friends.
- They do not need your approval for their friends.
- They are allowed to have opinions that may differ from yours.
- They are not accountable to you for every minute of their lives.
- They can be right from time to time (i.e., you don't have to be right all the time).

- They can win without you losing.
- They must be allowed to disagree with you, or anyone else.
- They have the right to not be constantly judged, belittled, and/or ridiculed by you.
- They have the right to self-respect.
- They should be allowed to be "normal."
- They should have personal time as a matter of normality, not privilege.
- They should be treated more kindly than co-workers.
- They should not have to experience or endure your vulgarity.
- They should not be the target for your misplaced anger.
- They should be able to be intimate with you, or not.

TRUE LOVE IS A SILENT LANGUAGE

While studying for my PhD at the American University, a class in family therapy exposed me to a concept attributed to a family therapist named Virginia Satir. The concept has influenced me ever since. Simply paraphrased, she said you cannot *not* communicate (Satir, Banmen, Gerber, and Gorman,1991).

This led to refreshing teaching points to provide to my audiences concerning changing and improving. I now encourage people to tell their loved ones they love them, without saying it! That means doing something (or not doing something) that will clearly indicate to someone your love for them. It may show them you are thinking of them, are sorry for a misdeed, desire to please them, want to be with them, miss them, appreciate them, and more. It may be as simple as picking up your clothes, helping with the kids' baths, or just being more thoughtful. It doesn't have to have a monetary value attached. It is easy to say, "I can't afford to bring home flowers all the time." This is often a copout. It doesn't cost a penny to be considerate, kind, thoughtful, or loving. Forget the flowers—it only takes you!

Another tip is being able to touch someone without putting your hands on them. It has been said people will forget what you say, and they will forget what you do, but rarely, if ever, will they forget how you make them feel.

Eventually, the partners in marriage share different values than each held at the time of their courtship and early days of marriage. The estimates I have seen regarding the amount of time husbands and wives spend communicating during the course of a week is always less than an hour, and usually much less. Healthy relationships/marriages are based upon satisfactory communication.

Regardless of whether police divorce rates are high, if officers and their spouses believe it is true, when marital problems occur, couples may simply bow to the inevitable and seek the divorce they expected to experience in the first place, instead of putting effort into solving their problems or seeking professional help. Only as a functioning component of the family can an officer participate in the furtherance of family plans, goals, and satisfaction.

If families are to succeed they will need "MAPS" to get where they are going. MAPS is an acronym used to describe the major components of a goal. Goals must be:

_____**M**easurable

_____**A**chievable

_____**P**ersonal

_____**S**pecific

Goals must be written with these four components included. All indications are that if goals are not written, they are not remembered, monitored, or achieved. An officer who has become detached from his family cheats them out of his input in family leadership, plans, and goals.

Honesty and trust are paramount if the relationship is to survive. Often in the lives of police officers, honesty is impossible based upon what they have experienced. Therefore, they come home, isolate themselves from family members, and say little if anything. When not using "police language," like "10-4," or "Roger that," little else is said.

Remember—you cannot not communicate. Thus, silence is a way of saying, "I can't talk to you about my day," but is often interpreted as, "I don't want to talk to you about my day." In time, the officer's values change and the changes are unnoticed due to the lack of sharing. While the police family has been the subject of numerous written works, absolute solutions for their problems have not yet become common in the literature (Reese & Scrivner, 1991). Police officers do not feel they can share their problems with anyone. They are expected to be able to solve everyone else's problems.

The power advantages in a marriage were once determined by gender, the husband being the dominant partner. It now appears to be an egalitarian system in which the person with the greatest resources gains the greatest power. A resource is defined as anything that one person brings to the marriage that helps satisfy the needs and goals of the other person. A henpecked husband is merely a man who has brought few resources to the marriage and thus is dominated by his wife. This gradual change signaled the death of the patriarchal tradition. Unfortunately, the stability of the American marriage is at greater risk than ever (based upon divorce statistics) and law enforcement officers fall into the same situations as others. Add to that the special stresses their families face and it can be assumed their efforts must be increased to allow for their marriage's survival. The major issues law enforcement officers continue to present to mental health professionals involve relationships and the impact of their jobs on those relationships.

In Cops Don't Cry (Stone, 1999), a police wife explores the experiences of police families. According to Stone, there are advantages to being married to a cop and they are as follows: security, it forces you to grow up, and you lead an exciting life. It is reported as never dull; you are married to someone who is honest and hardworking, and great in crisis. You get good benefits, and 85 percent of the wives surveyed said they would marry a cop again.

But too often, over time, we take our partners for granted. A friend of ours shared a story that summarizes how profound our need for communication can be. As a child her home also served as a funeral parlor. Due to her family business, they were constantly exposed to grieving spouses, other relatives, and friends. She recalls hearing time after time loving comments made to the deceased such as "I love you" and "How can I live without you?" She concluded with a moral to this story. "Too often the words we long to hear are whispered in the ears of the dead." The idea of cherishing life with each other is one that is embodied in her profound observation.

Marriages require maintenance. There are no manuals for marriage maintenance. It takes partners who are willing to communicate honestly and change when necessary for the common good. Effective maintenance must be performed regularly. Simple questions like "How are we doing?" "What do we see changing?" and "How can I make you like me more?" provide an atmosphere of honesty in a relationship and foster positive growth.

Solutions for police families suggest shift work requires a lifestyle plan, promotions can be stressful and not always a good thing, undercover work has very unique issues, and that the endless work, criticism, and pressure of being on call are things you accept. Fear of line-of-duty death is a persistent phenomenon in most police families. Change isn't easy in a police family, but perhaps coming to a realization that there is more to life than the badge may be a start.

5

POLICE PARENTS AND POLICE KIDS: STANDARD OPERATING PROCEDURES AT HOME

"HAND OVER THE REMOTE...NOW!"

A SON'S VIEW

Our boys now realize that Daddy is a police officer, and my older son, LJ, says he wants to be a police officer when he grows up. I wonder if he, at age seven, is trying to please us, but I'm sure he has an awareness of "bad guys" and being safe, more so than the neighbor's kids, whose Dad works in finance. LJ will dress up like a cop and tell us with a proud smile he saw someone suspicious so he stayed away. When the evening news shows cops shot or when we discuss Mark's work, we keep things from our kids to nullify their worry. Some nights when Mark is working late, LJ will ask me, "Why can't the bad guys be good so Daddy can come home?" I think about how many police wives do what I do as I try to explain that Daddy is making the world a better and safer place for everyone. My son LJ said the top three best things about having a cop as a dad were that he always feels safe, his dad is cool, and he has a fun and exciting life.

Cherie Castellano (2006)

A DAUGHTER'S VIEW

I tried to spend quality time with my daughter, Jamie. I can't remember ever wearing an FBI hat. I suppose I could have worn an FBI sweatshirt, or something else that identified me as an agent. I always chose not to. I never believed that what I did for a living really mattered to my child (although she tells me now how proud she is of me for what I did), or anyone else. What really mattered was that I spent time with her. In fact, when my daughter was very young, she was quoted as telling someone her daddy worked for IBM. I guess IBM and FBI are three initials that aren't so different from each other for a child so young. In retrospect, it appears I obviously did not emphasize to my young daughter what I did for a living. That wasn't important. My role with her was to be her dad, love her, teach her, make her feel safe, and guide her. In fact, later in life when asked what her dad's favorite pastime was, she responded, "My dad's favorite pastime is spending time with me." I knew that to be the truth; I'm glad she knew it too. That relationship hasn't changed to this day!

James T. Reese (1978)

Officers are accustomed to commands, orders, and directions, and are not apt to engage in discussions or make requests. Commanding and ordering spouses and children can create a tense and difficult environment in a law enforcement family. Many wives complain that their husbands sometimes speak to them as though they were criminals. Some children relate that their law enforcement officer parent can seem distant and difficult to approach. To separate the role of cop from that of parent or spouse is a monumental task at best and one that many law enforcement officers struggle with on a daily basis.

Research conducted by Vali Stone asked young people from ages ten to twenty-five to describe their greatest fear, which was the line-of-duty death of the police officer in their family (1999). When asked, they complained he or she was never home. Police kids think their discipline is a little tougher. Of the kids surveyed, more than 90 percent said they were proud their parent was a police officer. That's reassuring, but children should be proud of their parents regardless of their profession.

It is believed that one cannot love another without "giving of themselves." Instead, some officers have two and three jobs trying to provide their families with those things that "everyone else seems to have." New cars, bigger houses, trendy clothes for their kids, high-definition, flat-screen televisions, computer games, and the list goes on. Families rarely want what you can give them if they can't have you also. Therefore, you are the greatest gift you can give them.

Furthermore, officers protect their families from the tragedies they encounter by not talking about them. They begin to "protect" their families from the possibilities of being a victim of the very accidents they see and the crimes they investigate. Limitations are placed on the family. Late-night driving is not allowed; curfews are enforced to the minute; even pulling over for a "blue light" is cautioned by the officer because of the possibility of someone falsely portraying a police officer. A certain degree of concern for family safety is understandable. The extreme concern shown by officers, combined with their paranoia, tends to express a lack of support for family members and a lack of respect for the decisions they make concerning their own safety.

Law enforcement parents are either totally in command, or they totally relinquish the command to the partner. Successful marriages work jointly in decision making and discipline. The all-or-nothing approach has little value in keeping a relationship healthy or providing good role models for children concerning parenting. Fortunately, there are more positive than negative traits with which police fathers and mothers can influence their children. Having a parent who stands for law and order, is drug-free, is not a criminal, has dedicated his or her life to the betterment of society, and makes a steady income is very beneficial. One must focus on the good traits, because the fewer bad ones seem to get all the attention.

So, it appears change is in order. Unfortunately, change of any kind, even through structured family therapy, is stressful. Families have to be capable of dealing with it. The best way to do this is to identify the changes, and the impact these changes have had, and reevaluate the value of the changes. To simply change to accommodate another is less than satisfying and usually not permanent. A change must be purposeful and be of value to all involved in order to last.

In law enforcement, "power positions" can change. It has been said that if one is an officer prior to marriage, the relationship has a better chance of survival than if the husband or wife becomes an officer after marriage. Perhaps this is because they don't know what they are getting themselves into.

We must be realistic as well as optimistic. One officer said the job used to be what he did for a living. He sadly reported that he now does it for a life. What constitutes the issues in the life of a law enforcement officer? Here are a few of the issues facing law enforcement today:

- Long hours
- Dangerous assignments
- Everyday dangers
- The security of silence
- Unnecessary time away from home
- Use of alcohol and controlled substances
- Language and style of communication
- Priorities
- Friends
- Special assignments
- Authority and command
- Isolation of emotions
- Different view of "normal people"
- Judgmental attitude
- Negative attitude
- Inability or unwillingness to admit to mistakes
- Loyalty toward "others"
- Peacemaker image to others
- Immediate response to criticism
- Sarcasm and cynicism
- Holding one's children to a higher standard than other children
- Spouse's feelings of unimportance and being taken for granted
- Inability to deal with minor issues

Our personalities take on the following qualities after serving in law enforcement:

- Authoritative
- In command
- Intolerant of mistakes
- Possessing image armor
- Craving action
- Taking risks
- Hypervigilant
- Cynical
- Suspicious
- Less willing to socialize
- Regarding people negatively
- Not talking about feelings

Mental health professionals must remember these attributes and characteristics when providing psychological services to law enforcement personnel and their families. For example, police officers are expected to always be in control, to never be afraid, to always have solutions to other people's problems, and to not have any problems of their own. They view counseling as being for those not strong enough to help themselves.

Traditionally, police officers have avoided seeking assistance from mental health professionals. The reasons for this are two-fold: (1) They don't really believe that anyone else understands their problems, and (2) they have bought into the "hype" that police officers shouldn't have any problems. Thus, police officers have tended to turn to each other for help (an apparent endorsement for peer counseling but not a total rejection of "outside" help). The following are examples of statements emergency service professionals very rarely make: "I don't know," "I was wrong," "I need help," "I'm afraid," and "I made a mistake." Changes in the past few decades regarding police psychological services have lessened the resistance to seeking help, although it still persists in some agencies and with some officers.

A NEW DAY

The hardened attitudes officers develop to get through the workday are useful and accepted at work, but stand out dramatically and inappropriately at home. First, family members should be aware of being deliberately excluded from the officer's life. An example of this is when the officer identifies himself or herself primarily as a member of a closed law enforcement community and adopts the attitudes of "silence is security," "sex is survival," "always keep your cool," and "stay on top." Second, the spouse should see if the officer has increasing difficulty relating to members of the family or is less able to respond emotionally or talk about feelings. Third, the spouse should be on the lookout for an increase in anger and excessive use of several defense mechanisms, to include isolation of emotions and projection (blaming others).

Mental health professionals now look at the family as a system and as an extremely influential variable in the behavior of individuals. Law enforcement is also beginning to view its officers in the family setting. Although an integral part of any law enforcement agency has long been thought to be the individual officer, this concept is undergoing some modifications.

The family is now understood as an essential part of an officer's morale and attitude toward the job. There was a time when officers grew up in a culture that emphasized hard work, long hours, and total dedication to the job. Today, more and more officers are willing to give up material things for personal time.

We have learned that the family is not a cozy, static structure for rest and recuperation; it is dynamic and very much alive. Thus the family is a support system. It is a resource pool, drawn on selectively by the officer, for support in moving in a direction of his or her choice, leaving the officer stronger. The caution here is to educate the officer, and the police department, that the officer is also an integral part of the support system of others, namely family members. The police mentality can be dangerous to this balance of support.

Being a police officer is difficult. Being a member of a police officer's family may be even more difficult. Marriages are the most fragile relationships on the planet. There seems to be a need to name law enforcement officers as the most divorced population and a population of alcohol abusers. Whether this is true or not, the statistics that would universally confirm this are lacking. Maybe it is a myth, a belief that "never was true, and always will be."

COMPROMISING, UNDERSTANDING, AND COMMUNICATING

Many law enforcement officers are unable to explain to their loved ones the impact the job has on them, or the love they have for the job, even with all its shortcomings. For many, the job is what they do. For other less fortunate officers, the job is who they are. They come home and lose their identity. As police officers they use physical and mental distancing to remove themselves from the emotional punishment associated with their work. It soon becomes a part of their norm. Devices such as sunglasses, an impersonal tone of voice, and aloofness help to create distance. Officers must deal with their emotions and be cognizant of how they can negatively carry over to their own family.

THE DEFENSE NEVER RESTS

A catchy title for F. Lee Bailey's book (1971), this statement actually rings true in the law enforcement profession. The job of a law enforcement officer pushes and pulls from many directions, causing the officer to play the hard nut in one situation, and then move smoothly into the role of sympathetic helper in the next. Often he or she will choose to ignore, or unconsciously repress, the emotional problems of role conflict, ambiguity, and subsequent stress caused by "shifting gears" into the various roles they must play. In law enforcement, officers are constantly defending themselves from psychological damage. In addition to our intentional actions and thoughts to mitigate stress, much of this "mental protection" operates on a subconscious level via the previously discussed defense mechanisms.

Defense mechanisms arise as a response to stress, and become habituated through use. As the officer begins to succumb to the stress of the job, he or she begins to perceive that the offenders are winning, that everything meaningful is slipping out of reach, that the family is upset, and that he or she doesn't seem to care about the public. On the basis of these perceptions, behavior and attitudes are altered to make them less threatening. In other words, the officer adopts defense mechanisms.

Not only is there rapid change, the changes are more immediate in our culture than ever before. Institutions such as schools and places of worship once had substantial influence on adults and children alike. Today, they appear to be no longer revered by either. Their influence upon American families appears minimal at best. Many believe that the family as we knew it is disappearing (Kirschman, 1997). It becomes our challenge to be an ingredient in the glue that holds our families together.

An important concept to grasp, and educate our families about, is simply that we are not in control: not of our environment, our assignments, our hours, or the situations we find ourselves in. We ought to tell our families from the very beginning that "we are not self-employed." None of us is in a position to deny reporting for duty when asked. Once asked, the answer is a given. We are sworn to be on duty, to be ready to respond to commands and serve, 24 hours a day, seven days a week. Cops know this "24-7" means their lives will be consistently interrupted during their careers.

That means we must act with integrity every day of our careers. Others may be able to say in response to a phone ringing, "If that's for me, tell them I'm not here." It is shameful to imagine a public servant such as a law enforcement officer asking a family member to do that. Instead, we answer the phone, report for duty, and disappoint the family that depended on us being home that night. Missing birthdays, working on holidays, and irregular hours are the norm. We cause our spouses to take on the role of single parents.

Unfortunately, during the course of an officer's career, changes take place. These changes can be acute, such as experiencing tragedy, or chronic, such as the day-to-day rigors and exposure to pain and suffering, being lied to, and living on the edge. Eventually, the officer may not answer the phone, justifying the action by asking, "What have they (the department) done for me after all my years of service?"

When one combines all these factors, and adds to them the daily influence of other officers, the change can be inevitable at times. However, it doesn't have to take up permanent residence in your life. A police officer can be a model husband and an excellent officer. Most are, but it is up to you to determine if you are one of them. If you are not, you have the solution to that problem, no one else.

SPECIAL CONSIDERATIONS DURING SPECIAL CIRCUMSTANCES

Children can become anxious, confused, or frightened when exposed to an officer's world, so it is important to give children guidance that will help them minimize their fears. Children depend on daily routines: They wake up, eat breakfast, go to school, and play with friends. When a trauma or disaster occurs, this routine is interrupted and those children can become anxious. They will look to you and other adults for help. Your law enforcement family may have to leave home and interrupt or alter their daily routine. As a law enforcement officer, you have the advantage of understanding emergency responses and should be able to provide guidance for your family during the crisis.

If you react with alarm, a child may become more scared; when you are calm, they will follow your lead. They see our fear as proof the danger is real. If you seem overcome with a sense of loss the child may feel their losses more intensely. Children's fears often stem from their imaginations and you should take these feelings seriously. A child who feels afraid is afraid, and your words and actions can provide reassurance despite the real danger.

When speaking with your child, present a realistic picture that is both honest and manageable. Feelings of fear are normal and natural for adults and children, but as an adult you need to keep control of the situation. When you are sure the danger has passed, concentrate on your child's emotional needs. Have children participate in the family's recovery activities, as this can also help them feel they are regaining control of their normal life. Your response during these times will have a lasting impact. Be aware that after a crisis or disaster, children are most afraid the event will happen again, someone will be injured or killed, they will be separated from their family, and/or they will be left alone.

Start with the basics. Teach your child how to recognize danger signals. Make sure your child knows what smoke detectors, fire alarms, and local community warning systems sound like. Explain how to call for help. Teach your child how and when to call for help. Check the telephone directory for local emergency numbers and post these numbers by all telephones. If you live in a 9-1-1 service area, tell your child when to call 9-1-1. Even very young children can be taught how and when to call for emergency assistance. Help your child memorize important family information. They should also know where to meet in case of an emergency. They should carry a small index card that lists emergency information to give to an adult or a babysitter.

As a law enforcement family, some advice to parents is simple. Create a family disaster plan and practice it so everyone in your family feels prepared and in control as much as possible. When something occurs, you will feel the advantage of that preparation. Teach your child how to participate in the disaster plan. Everyone in the household should play a part in your family's response or recovery efforts in times of need. After the disaster, it is a time for recovery and immediately time to reduce your child's fear and anxiety. Much of this is done by talking about the circumstances and letting the child talk.

Keep the family together. You may initially want to have your children with relatives or friends. If possible, keep the family together as much as possible and make children a part of what you are doing to get the family back on its feet. Children get anxious and they will get worried that their parents won't return if they are separated from them. Calmly and firmly explain the situation as best you can. Explain what will happen next. For example, say, "Tonight we will all stay together." Get down to the child's eye level and use easily understandable language.

Encourage children to talk. Let children talk about the issue and ask questions as much as they choose. Encourage children to describe what they are feeling and listen to what they say. If possible include the entire family. Reassure them with firmness and love. Your child will realize that life will eventually return to normal. If a child does not respond to the above suggestions, seek help from a mental health specialist, member of the clergy, or pediatrician.

There are some things police officers can do with their families to maintain a police family life that is healthy. Create your own "Law Enforcement Family Code of Ethics" (Stone, 1999), laying out rules and responsibilities, which are always important in any group unit, particularly your family. (See Appendix C.) Adapt this format in whatever style and language best meets your needs. The simple act of using this tool to clarify your needs and goals may be a profound step in the right direction.

6

TRAUMA IN POLICE WORK

"VALOR WOULD CEASE TO BE A VIRTUE, IF THERE WERE NO INJUSTICE."

AGESILAUS THE GREAT, GREEK KING OF SPARTA (455 BC–361 BC)

The first post-critical-incident interview I conducted has had a far-reaching effect upon my opinion that post-critical-incident care must be a nonnegotiable mandate in law enforcement. The notoriety of this case focused on a young, and obviously disturbed, man named Charles Whitman. In 1966 Whitman killed his wife and his mother and left a note admitting his confused state of mind.

Following these murders, he climbed the tower at the University of Texas at Austin and began shooting indiscriminately at people below. Within 90 minutes he had killed more than a dozen passersby and wounded more than two dozen. It wasn't until an off-duty deputy sheriff climbed the tower and killed Whitman that the slaughter came to an end.

During my interview with this deputy sheriff, fourteen years following the incident, I learned there was no psychological help offered to him or his family. Admittedly, this was not unusual during the '60s. The fact remained that the disturbance in Whitman's life ended that day, while the disturbances in the lives of the officers at the scene began. The impact on family was apparent during the interview and little was known about how to "get the family back to normal."

FBI Special Agent James T. Reese (1978)

For the next three decades I saw, and still continue to see, the gradual, yet gratifying, mental transition in law enforcement officers from an attitude of "my family will have to live with it" to "I have to find a way to live with my family." The most current issues surround the efforts of law enforcement personnel, and others, at the World Trade Center (terrorism), New Orleans (natural disaster), Virginia Tech (mass murder), and more. From Manhattan to New Orleans, Madrid to Maui, Brisbane to Baltimore, law enforcement officers continue to respond to tragedies and are emotionally altered during each response.

I'M NOT THE COP I USED TO BE

Of the many hazards challenging the emotional well-being of law enforcement officers, their most formidable foe may well be their response, and subsequent reactions, to critical incidents. This is not meant to discount the impact day-to-day stress has on law enforcement officers. However, when one combines these everyday emotional issues with critical incidents, it becomes obvious that law enforcement officers continue to be an "at-risk" population for emotional and physical pain. Even when "normal" psychological adjustment has occurred, there is a high probability there will be some degree of continuing disequilibrium within the officer and, subsequently, his or her family.

It should be noted that all professions risk having someone die on the job. The difference lies in the fact that job-related deaths, for the most part, are accidental. Police officers are murdered. This constant stress, together with the possibilities of the stress of unrealistic management, poor leadership, little or no specialized training, long hours, often less pay than deserved, dangerous situations, shift work, working on holidays, lack of gratitude, responding to the unknown, and being on duty every minute of every day, creates changes in officers. These changes are gradual but oftentimes lethal to intimate relationships. The gradual nature of these changes usually means the officer is blind regarding them. They are seen by others and denied by him.

Vicarious victims

An officer does not have to witness violence or death to suffer the potential hazards of critical incidents. As evidence of this, in 1987 I was invited to King County, Washington, to speak to the Green River Murders Task Force on the topics of stress and burnout. This presentation, as well as my presentation to the Tylenol Task Force in Chicago, exposed them to the reality of the fragile family and stresses faced by officers. They were torn between long hours demanded of them at work due to their perceived responsibility to the public, and the demands of family to not spend so much time at work. Officers and their families suffer, albeit silently, long after cases have been solved.

Every day of officers' lives, they are like "human sponges." They soak in the emotional pain of others, insults, feelings of helplessness, perceived lack of fairness in life, and other matters of despair. How does an officer who has just witnessed violence, brutality, and even death come home and be warm, sensitive, and loving? Society expects law enforcement officers to be able to cope with the demands of the job and to be able to turn their emotions on and off at will.

The police function is unique, in that officers respond on a routine basis to calls which those not in the police profession would consider emergencies. It has been stated that the police profession may not be all that dangerous physically, but it is perhaps the most emotionally dangerous job in existence. With this in mind, and adding to that the lack, or in some cases imagined lack, of public support, families and peers have become an absolutely essential resource in maintaining and enhancing the mental well-being of law enforcement officers.

You are exposed so often in this police career to traumatic events that we must differentiate among the possible traumas. The basic definition of critical-incident stress is a normal response to an abnormal event. What is a critical incident? Critical-incident stress can be connected to a highly publicized event, death or injury of an officer, mass causality, death of a child, AIDS, hazardous materials issue, inmate suicide or officer suicide or other suicide. We know there are physical, behavioral, emotional, and cognitive reactions to critical incidents and the signs of obvious distress are the chest pains, decreased sleep, angry outbursts, depression, hopelessness, confused thinking, and difficulty in making decisions (Everly and Castellano, 2005).

There are critical incidents in which you are emotionally involved and feeling human emotions. Professionals in the mental health field now refer to "compassion fatigue," which relates to how you experience exposure to human suffering while at work. Compassion fatigue is the emotional residue of the exposure of allowing yourself to feel on the job, which may become a liability for you (Figley, 1995). Compassion fatigue symptoms are very subtle. Your job performance will go down, your morale will drop, and your personal relationships will be affected in a serious way. At times you may even require a medical leave due to a decline in physical health.

Literature on suicidal police officers has provided suggestions that trauma has an impact, over time, on police officers and their families. The everyday coping tactics used by some officers may not be ideal. It is not ideal to drink or take drugs. It is not ideal to think you are alone. It is not ideal to have unrealistic recovery expectations or angry outbursts. Ideally you may utilize two primary functions for critical-incident stress. Those two functions are stabilization and working through the issue (Paton, Douglas, and Violanti, 2006).

If you have been involved in a critical incident, talk about the incident with a critical-incident-stress specialist (peer), licensed clinician, or member of the clergy. If properly trained, they can help you process the incident and identify the traumatic effects the event has had upon you, if any. Expect it may bother you, so allow yourself to take some time off. Get accurate information and feedback about the incident. Learn about critical-incident stress, post-traumatic stress disorder, eye movement desensitization and reprocessing (EMDR) therapy, and other tools that may be helpful for critical-incident stress.

In terms of 'working through' a trauma, labeling an event and encouraging a self-inventory process may allow for an opportunity to rewrite your basic beliefs. Your basic beliefs are the "shoulds" in your life based on your early experiences. When you have a traumatic event in your life it may challenge your beliefs, and your faith in God, humanity, and your world. Rewrite those basic beliefs in a way that is healing and can be integrated with your real-life family story.

Survival tactics with kids are simply monitoring them. What are you going to watch for in your kids after a critical incident in an officer's life? Temper tantrums, aches and pains, guilt and responsibility, bedtime troubles for the little ones, school phobias and problems for the older ones. Avoidant or aggressive behavior may be a subtle sign a police kid is a vicarious victim. Get in touch with the family dynamics and recognize that you can reassure your child openly and model healthy behavior on how to cope with feeling like a victim.

UNIQUE ASSIGNMENTS AND ROLES

One must ask, "Is this job what I do, or is it who I am?" If the job is what you do, you have a better chance of doing something else when you are off duty. If the job is, in fact, who you are, your chances of being a family man are diminished. It is important to remember there are those among us who simply cannot let go of the image and authority, even off duty. They continually dress in some form of police attire, or wear clothes that represent the profession. From T-shirts promoting the police unions to SWAT jackets and caps with badges, they must be recognized for who they are, namely, cops.

Law enforcement officers are seldom heard saying, "I made a mistake," "I'm wrong," 'I need help," "or "I'm afraid." Too often in the history of law enforcement, these phrases were seen as signs of weakness. We have learned that, in actuality, the weak may be the ones who refuse to admit problems, and/or chastise those who would ask for "help." The strong come to a realization at some point that it is OK to seek help, to make efforts to allow others to help you, and to admit it's OK to not be OK all the time.

Ask the question in the solitude of your mind. Is your job your life, or the way you make a living? Can you stop being a cop long enough each day to be part of your family? If not, history will prove that your family will grow without you, separate from you, until you are no longer emotionally attached to them. And, without emotional attachment, you are no different than any other person they encounter during their lives. This is often followed by physical detachment, namely separation or divorce.

The rules of life vary with every individual. Challenges are always present in trying to apply the rules to life. A couple of good rules by which to live your life may be (1) Nothing comes before the God I believe in, and (2) I will try to avoid knowingly doing anything that will bring dishonor to my family or myself. Humans are far from perfect, but rules at least help us stay focused. Discover the rules in your life. If you come up empty-handed, create some. Share your rules with someone you care for. Reinvent yourself if necessary and appropriate!

In the last few years, agencies across the country have started programs to assist officers in surviving the tumultuous aftermath of a shooting. Many law enforcement officers have used deadly force and, in retrospect, reflect that the media frenzy, legal system, department scrutiny, public criticism, and psychological shock are more traumatic than the actual shooting. Statistics reflect that almost one third of the officers involved in deadly force incidents are able to return to work without experiencing problems. The majority, however, need assistance from a mental health professional, department debriefing, peer support group, clergy member, or some other resource to help them return to normal after the trauma of taking another person's life. Too often the law enforcement officer's family members are not considered. Law enforcement families get lost in all the chaos surrounding the shooter. They do, however, have to contend with the fear and shock of knowing that a loved one has experienced a life-threatening event.

Many officers will relate stories in their post-shooting lives in which their spouse suddenly struggled as they left for work or became sentimental or emotional every time they were away from the family. As with law enforcement officers, law enforcement families will respond differently after an incident or shooting. Their response may depend on how the individual family dynamics and preparation factored into the law enforcement family before and after the incident. Some law enforcement officers and their families will bounce back quickly, while others may be devastated. Since law enforcement family members can develop post-traumatic stress disorder, it is important to understand and receive assessment in and education about trauma reactions to these critical incidents.

The love and empathy family members feel for each other is often the rock they stand on to survive a deadly force encounter. While there is no question police officers and their significant others can benefit from counseling, it is important that we recognize the struggle to trust others outside the family in the context of these types of incidents. Officers and their families may be reluctant to discuss the gory details of this type of event and their reaction to it. Members of the family may be reluctant to discuss their anxiety. This anxiety often brings their ultimate fear—line-of-duty death—to the forefront. Everyone in the law enforcement family involved in a shooting incident will attempt to protect each other and struggle to support each other to survive.

As with anything else it is important for law enforcement family members to respect individual differences in how each person copes with this type of traumatic event. Law enforcement officers sometimes wonder how much, when, or in what context to speak to their children. Many factors contribute to these decisions, including age, maturity, and temperament.

As a rule of thumb, relay the facts in a calm, neutral, reassuring manner and ask whether the child has any questions. Children will let you know how much they need to understand by the nature of their questions. Keep the lines of communication open and look for any changes in behavior. Counseling and assessments are always an option if problems seem to be developing after a period of time. To prepare your law enforcement family members for this type of incident, you should be concerned over their reactions to your involvement in a shooting incident.

There are many options for a law enforcement officer. Prepare ahead of time, making a plan as to what each person will do, such as, Who will notify other family and friends, and how? Who will go to be with the officer and who will wait at home? Who will look after the children? To minimize uncomfortable surprises the family should be familiar with all that may happen after a shooting—typical media response, criminal investigation, grand jury, and possible civil litigation.

Virginia Satir, an experiential family therapist, stated that "communication is to relationships what breathing is to life" (Satir, Banmen, Gerber, and Gorman,1991). The quality of interactions with spouses in law enforcement is often sorely lacking. They can be of short duration, sporadic, and with faulty or impure communication. The couple grows apart, leaving the spouse of the officer feeling unimportant and often rejected. How can a law enforcement officer switch roles after eight hours of being a cop, especially if he or she has just watched someone die?

Open communication is essential inside and outside the family in these times of crisis. It is a police-involved shooting incident that can also move us together to our faith, our unity, and our recognition that our law enforcement families are our safest unit.

7

DISASTER RECOVERY: POLICE RESILIENCE

"A HERO IS NO BRAVER THAN AN ORDINARY MAN, BUT HE IS BRAVER FIVE MINUTES LONGER."
RALPH WALDO EMERSON

"SUPERHUMAN POWERS"

September 11, 2001, had an impact on my family in ways that I can never fully explain. My husband worked the bucket brigade at Ground Zero and the streets of Jersey City where a lot of activity occurred post 9/11. I worked at Ground Zero as a counselor for police officers and remained there providing direct services for several months. Seeing death in massive numbers, especially of cops, a fear began to surface that I had never known. What I also recognized is that with both of us involved in different ways in this disaster, my husband helped me tremendously but I was too drained to help him. How ironic, an alleged expert in counseling officers involved in 9/11 and I did not help my own husband the way I should have. He forgave me, we used our faith, and we got through it. From that point on, our police family had a darker tone. Now our kids and families know cops get killed, the world is a dangerous place, and we depend on our police officers' "superhuman powers" to protect us and them. Every year on 9/11 I pray for the officers who died and those who heroically served our nation in the rescue and recovery from that horrible disaster, and the families left behind.

In addition I pray for the 9/11 officer "survivor" families who also lost moments, birthdays, dinners, meals, holidays, baseball games, and Christmas concerts. These are lost moments that may never be regained. May the Lord bless them with an abundance of new moments together in years to come without disasters to balance the scales of sacrifice and love.

Cherie Castellano (2002)

Disaster preparedness has become a way of life for many U.S. law enforcement professionals participating in elite units responsible for security, rescue, and recovery during a mass disaster. Critical-incident stress is an everyday part of the job as a law enforcement officer. In this "new normal" related to mass disasters and terrorism, our world is further changed. Officers may be identified in the police family as "survivor victims" (Everly and Castellano, 2005). We know what to do when an officer is killed in the line of duty. National organizations, governments, and communities have emerged to honor and recognize the ultimate sacrifice in law enforcement known as line-of-duty death. How should we cope with officers who were not killed in a mass disaster but are "forever gone"? Many police spouses whose officers survived September 11th say they (the spouses) are dramatically changed. How do we handle "acute traumatic stress" as a law enforcement family?

"Rescuer survivor victims" of terrorism can resort to basic elements similar to counterterrorism tactics. One can psychologically "build up" resilience and be able to counter the impacts of terrorism, known as "psychological counterterrorism" (Everly and Castellano, 2005). The core elements are to understand the nuances of terrorism, understand who you are with a psychological risk assessment, and get organizational and leadership support, along with a psychological critical-incident stress management service component. The "ten commandments of psychological survival" for law enforcement families can be incorporated into your lives. (See Appendix E.)

"Shattered assumptions of safety" is described as an experience that is available now for a subsample of people who have been victimized by terrorism in their state or community (Brewin and Holmes, 2003). They will always see themselves as available to be revictimized. A psychological risk assessment may uncover an officer's personal vulnerability to trauma.

In the year 2000 a study was done reviewing differences in individual trauma reactions related to three primary vulnerabilities: biological, historical, and psychological. It showed that biologically, if you are someone who tends to get chest pains or panic attacks or are in poor health, you are obviously vulnerable to physical deterioration related to trauma. Historically, if you have been a victim of crime or been abused in your early life, you may be vulnerable to trauma. Psychologically, to simplify clinical terms, if you are abusing alcohol, anxious, thinking about cheating on your wife, or on the verge of an angry outburst, trauma exposure may push you over the edge.

In assessing your personal vulnerability to trauma, be aware of your brother and sister officers in your rank and file who may be vulnerable (Everly and Castellano, 2005). In contrast, some officers are actually enhanced by intense assignments and dangerous responses. Called a "positive growth model," psychologists describe positive outcomes for first responders, who may actually have a post-traumatic growth in three categories in their lives (Tedeschi and Calhoun, 1996). The three areas for growth are identified by officers who describe themselves as better, their relationships as enhanced, and their spiritual and religious sense as intensified. They don't simply survive the traumatic event and go home to their family. Certain types of officers may actually experience themselves as better than they were before and see the trauma as an opportunity to grow as a person. Law enforcement families hope for an officer with this type of resistance and resilience.

Data was gathered from interviews with approximately one hundred urban search and rescue team members from September 11th who were assigned to ten days of rescue and recovery (Castellano, Nestor and Mascioli, 2005). The three most stressful aspects of the job following September 11th were the loss of life, family matters, and their family's safety and relationships.

Positive coping skills to deal with this trauma in a mass disaster response included talking with co-workers. Spending time with their family members post-event was reported as the second most important support. Negative coping skills to deal with the stress of the event were frequently reported as withdrawal and isolation, alcohol, and excessive anger.

Law enforcement leadership can alter how your law enforcement family is impacted. Grief leadership can be demonstrated as appropriate sadness and reactions that reflect a mental link to the loss of life and acknowledge the loss. Leaders should model positive behaviors, communicating with subordinates in the aftermath of a trauma, holding memorial services, and expressing grief as important tools to wellness. Leaders should also recognize the impact these events have on both the officer and his family members.

Officers consistently report that mental health programs can be informative and useful. Trauma from natural disasters reflects a need for control in personal preparedness and family closeness. Officers described awareness and appreciation of their surroundings and personal humility when all is lost.

Separation from family is often described as a stressor. Trauma from man-made disasters reflects an officer's experience focused on anger and helplessness as primary stressors.

Anecdotal information from critical-incident stress management group interactions in Psychological Counterterrorism & World War IV supports that officers had four primary emotions and four primary behaviors attached to those emotions in response to September 11th (Everly & Castellano, 2005). Anger was the predominant emotion expressed: anger at their helplessness, as an expression of grief, at the terrorists, at the magnitude and innocence of those lost. Grief was the second most frequently expressed emotion, as many fellow officers were killed and/or injured in this horrific event—grief over the mass casualties and the morbidity of the circumstances of their deaths. The third emotion, depression, was related to the first two emotions, anger and grief, but also connected to a loss of security forever.

Isolation marked the fourth most commonly expressed emotion because there were those who were there and those who were not there. A civilian who was not there could never understand what occurred. A law enforcement officer would not share that experience and it is considered a sacred experience to honor those lost never to be discussed lightly or in conversation with the civilian world. That left officers feeling isolated from the rest of the world because they chose to isolate themselves. They shared an experience together, much like the military, that by surviving it caused them to be in some way defined by it.

The officers' behaviors connected to their emotions followed a consistent pattern in officers involved in the events of September 11th. Hypervigilance at work was a behavioral attempt to feel effective at work and enabled officers an opportunity to overcome their feelings of helplessness. Doing something—anything—was better than doing nothing. That hypervigilance caused family discord, however. A spouse keeping the home together while an officer is working six days a week feels hurt when the officer volunteers to work on the seventh day as well. Agitation and arguments may ensue, fostering a cycle of family discord giving the officer an excuse to go back to work.

On a positive note officers joined together and formed work group cohesion in times of crisis. Politics and competition were secondary to accomplishing the mission as a cohesive unit. Most significantly for police families in the context of September 11th, law enforcement officers faced their mortality saying, "There but for the grace of God go I" and "Why did God spare me and take another officer's life?"

If an officer escaped from the building and was saved, he may reexamine his life. Officers suddenly decided to lose twenty pounds, reconnect with their wife, slow down on the drinking, or go to see their son's baseball game instead of working every day. Every moment became a precious moment because it could be their last. The self-inventory in which officers engaged was a positive experience for their law enforcement families. Most officers directly involved in September 11th and their wives and families benefited from the self-inventory as the crisis provided an opportunity for growth.

When all was said and done the unthinkable for some law enforcement officers occurred. Some realized they no longer wanted to be in police work. September 11th defined a new path for them that did not involve rescue or recovery. Perhaps the self-inventory for those officers reflected "Enough is enough" and they chose a new life.

Some officers decided to plan retirement early and begin focusing their energies on their families. Some families fell apart under the strain of the hours and trauma struggling with increases in alcohol abuse and aggression at home. Intimacy seemed hard to establish with many officers and their spouses. Intimacy was more prevalent in their police families post–September 11th if a foundation was set. A unity with those in the police family at work involved in the September 11th response was profound and intimate in many aspects. No spouse or child at home could relate to that unity of having survived the disaster and rescue/recovery efforts together.

Some spouses described feeling "left out" of the closeness shared between officers and their colleagues at work. Most leaders and elite rescuers who had experienced trauma before September 11th reported a closeness with their families based on a newfound sense of appreciation. I wonder how many spouses and children experienced that appreciation directly. Perhaps it was more of a thought than an action in most law enforcement families.

Family support services for rescuer survivor victims are never an easy endeavor. Schedules, kids, work, locations, something can always keep the spouse and kids separate from the officer. Perhaps that is not a coincidence, but part of a larger norm in police families that reflects an attitude of protecting officer family members by not disclosing or including them in anything related to traumatic work. If an officer witnessed a child's death or mass casualty scene and shares it with their significant other, it will be too upsetting, so instead, officers remain quiet, a couch potato, or "check out emotionally."

Most wives say they know instinctively their husbands are disturbed or haunted by an incident by their silence, demeanor, energy level, or behavior. Therefore we play the guessing game, "What was it?" "How should I approach him on it?" or the twenty questions game: "How was your day?" "Anything happen you want to talk about?" "You seem upset or quiet." Then we wait.

In the past six years, September 11th has been discussed by officers and their families as something that has changed their lives forever. Some officers realize that their dedication to the job, combined with an awareness of their feelings, allowed them to emotionally survive. Other officers are not aware of how they got through it without emotional scars. Regardless, their families are grateful for their survival, and are aware of what could have been.

God bless the families who lost officers in the events of September 11th. God bless the countless members of the clergy who comforted our officers when we, as spouses or friends, could not find the right words. Let us recognize our service in standing by our spouses as partners surviving September 11th. Let's forget our attempts to describe where Daddy was, or why, but even though we want our children to live in a world where terrorism is not an issue, we have to educate them about it particularly because of our spouses' profession

NATURAL DISASTERS

Looking for "higher ground" post-Hurricane Katrina sharply demonstrates the contrasts between man-made disasters and natural disasters, and the impact on police officers and their families (Castellano, Ussery, and Gruntfest, 2006).

A Louisiana resident reported that Katrina means "cleansing." Despite some negative media, the "cleansing" of Louisiana by law enforcement professionals and those officers deployed from around the country reflects endless acts of heroism and survival in the aftermath of Katrina. The effects of Hurricane Katrina are both a complex and varied experience, as most southern law enforcement professionals and their families were simultaneously both rescuers and victims of this horrific disaster.

The nature of the disaster was threefold: first, the actual natural disaster—the storm and flooding; second, the organizational crisis of the agencies responding; and, third, the personal crisis of the law enforcement officers involved in rescue and recovery and their families.

Some police officers allegedly barricaded their stations to avoid snipers and resorted to looting for shoes, dry socks, and food. Reports of carjackings, murders, thefts, and rapes flooded the news, but many of the stories were determined to likely be based on rumors.

The organizational crisis held implications surrounding preparedness and practical response for rescue and recovery. Planning appeared nonexistent and impromptu attempts at logistics were no competition for the wrath of the storm. Equipment and facility resources were limited by a variety of factors that warranted untraditional and often atypical adaptations of operations. Circumstances were unfathomable and, without a base of operation or command center, all "standard operating procedures" seemed obsolete.

The law enforcement group cohesion met expectations for emergency service personnel after surviving a mass disaster. Although they had generally grown closer together, there were some fracture lines between different shifts, superior officers, and those few officers who had left to take care of their families (even though they ultimately returned). Other reactions included justifiable anger, frustration, a feeling of abandonment, and hopelessness for recovery. They were in need of continued support during these difficult times until a greater sense of normalcy and stabilization could be established, including basic safety needs, housing, and clean clothes. Each law enforcement unit experienced different types of crises in their service, yet the thread of survival through faith always tied them together.

The personal crisis faced by these brave men and women responding to Hurricane Katrina as rescuer survivor victims fostered group cohesion, as they are "their brother's keeper." When attempts to rescue an officer are thwarted, a natural phenomenon of helplessness can occur, prompting a personal and family crisis.

Police survival techniques, in an environment of chaos, reflect a primary need, such as safety and security, as described in Maslow's Hierarchy of Needs (1943). On an individual basis, the personal crisis for law enforcement officers in response to Hurricane Katrina was profound. It was characterized by a basic conflict between their sworn oath to serve and protect the public and their human need to serve and protect their families.

The personal dilemma of law enforcement officers, either feeling they let down their police department or their police families, was obviously a "no-win" situation, with limited capacity to see their victimization in the process. Overwhelmingly, the efforts of the Louisiana law enforcement officers were heroic in that their focus was most often on rescue and recovery at the expense of their own health, safety, and mental health and well-being, defining the term "selfless." Unfortunately, the media depicted officers fraught with problems rather than tell the real stories of heroism post-Hurricane Katrina. Perhaps we needed, as a society or community, to direct our anger at specific groups, even despite the real activity of the majority of their members.

The denial required to go on at times like this, and the need to sustain this denial over such a long time period, makes this "recovery" (physical, psychological, etc.) a journey through cumulative stress reactions. Law enforcement officers who've lost everything must continue to care for their families and continue their to fulfill their duty to the community they serve. Therein lies the persistent struggle.

Perhaps law enforcement, "front line" first responders, can prepare in the future by asking themselves essential questions should they face the dilemma found in the response to Hurricane Katrina. How will you choose when faced with protecting your family or protecting others? What will be the implications for your career and your relationships pending that choice? What level of death and destruction will cause you to rethink your role? Maybe the answers can be found in building resiliency or simply recognizing the strengths you have functioned with thus far.

Most police officers have two entirely different but hopefully connected families. The police family is generally the group of officers who become friends within a specific unit an officer is tasked to work within. That unit functions as a family, sometimes dysfunctional, but the commitment to the individuals and the unit is intense and genuine, and reflects an intimacy of true friendships and "having each other's back."

The primary police family, the "real" law enforcement family, is the one the officer comes home to, to receive comfort, safety, and unconditional love. It is important that these two families don't compete openly, but in fact support each other. We must recognize that the law enforcement officer whom we share is an essential to both "units."

Resilience, faith, and a clear understanding of your value system and commitment levels are the way to push through a crisis of this magnitude. Law enforcement families were not factored into a plan to ensure and secure safety and peace of mind for the officers. Prior to another event like Hurricane Katrina, officer family plans and preparedness drills and contingencies must be established to ensure safety and the capacity to serve. Just considering these scenarios will at least allow you to think about your final decisions in response to disaster.

It is clear, as a law enforcement professional, your public service is "in your blood." Your heroism is inspirational, but you risk becoming the one of the victims you set out to rescue in mass disaster responses! And your life and family are just as valuable as the civilians you rescue.

Within a strong law enforcement family there seem to be attributes imperative to your survival that consistently reflect a resilient unit with adaptive ability. Consistent caring and appreciating of each other's service, when the rest of the world seems like they do not appreciate your efforts, is essential. Clear roles and responsibilities are key, as they may change in the course of shifts, jobs, and critical incidents on a regular basis. Commitment as a couple to communication with your children and your God remains a necessary constant.

Community and family ties that support all of you within the schools, the churches, neighborhood, and extended family must be utilized. Discover the family strengths you normally rely on, and actually set goals for yourselves as a family looking forward to happy and joyous times. Maintain your spirituality and time together to practice your faith while encouraging each other by sharing positive statements regularly. Perform activities that enhance your family as you would train your police unit. Some guidelines for law enforcement families in disaster can be established as a resource. (See Appendix A.)

Disaster preparedness should become a priority for your law enforcement family at home. Plan family disaster drills, review workplace, county, and state emergency management plans, and pray together, as you prepare to get through the next disaster. Law enforcement officers throughout the country are responding to human suffering caused by terrorism and disaster. A comment from Helen Keller in 1912 reflects their mission. She stated, in essence, that although the world is full of suffering, it is also full of overcoming it.

8

REINVENT YOURSELF—
SIX KEYS TO STRESS-FREE LIVING™

COMBINING THE PRESSURES OF WORK, THE PLEASURE OF FAMILY, AND THE POWER OF LOVE

There are strategies and attitudes that will help us, both at home and on the job, to limit unnecessary stress while increasing our productivity at work and enjoyment in our personal lives. Stress doesn't have to be bad. In fact, it has no meaning in our lives until we attach meaning to it. Learning to use stress to our advantage will separate us from the masses. Largely, it is our response to stimuli that influences our behavior.

Achieving at work, meeting all the deadlines, and earning all the bonuses will never be enough to ensure that one is successful. Today's marketplace is highly competitive and demanding and will only present more deadlines. It is full of people of exceptional talent, just like you, who seek advancements and rewards. Yet many of these individuals have let the stress of their jobs, and of life in general, work against them. It has been said that these individuals have "permanent potential" and "a major in minors." If you wish to effect a change in your world, you must change your attitudes. You don't have to give up happiness in order to have success.

We often live in prisons of our own fashioning. We have to eliminate these self-imposed limits. The power, which propels our future, is within us. The only limits are those of vision. Too often, we look for that power elsewhere. Many talented and motivated people simply stand by and "wait for a break," that "streak of luck," that "once-in-a-lifetime" opportunity. They will fall behind the pack. In reality, each day is an opportunity. Realizing that most of us get "stuck" at some point in our lives, and realizing that life is full of crossroads, which blend opportunity and risk, we must act responsibly and make educated choices.

Learn to live in the present. The greatest mistake a person can make is to be afraid of making a mistake. Don't lament about what could have been. Don't wait for tomorrow to begin self-appraisal, a personal inventory of what makes you feel the way you do. Do it now! What we eat, how we behave, our reactions, who we like, love and dislike, what we feel, who we become, our habits of exercise and relaxation, and more, determine our feelings, and, to a large degree, determine our longevity. They are all based upon choices we make.

Why has mankind chosen to ignore all the rules of nature? What is it about our belief system that allows us to act so arrogantly? Many of us believe we have been given dominion over all the other animals on the planet. They are all subject to the laws of nature and of their individual societies. Their behaviors are expected and predictable, from migration to mating. They understand the food chain and live within it, without compromise. They face challenges each day without self-pity and survive solely on their knowledge of the laws that govern them and their species. This has been quoted time and time again in the essence of survival:

Every morning in Africa, a gazelle wakes up. It knows it must run faster than the fastest lion or it will be killed . . . Every morning a lion wakes up. It knows it must outrun the slowest gazelle or it will starve to death. It doesn't matter whether you are the lion or the gazelle. . . when the sun comes up, you'd better be running.

There are laws that govern our existence. These laws are of divine origin, and we are required to understand them and live by them. Not until we get this big picture will we understand that we are rapidly causing our own demise. We must also begin to concern ourselves with the **Six Keys to Stress-Free Living™**, namely (1) challenge, (2) choice, (3) change, (4) courage, (5) control, and (6) commitment, if we are to improve the quality of our lives, individually and collectively. The distance between success and failure will be measured by our desire.

KEY ONE

The first key to consider is that of challenge. Law enforcement officers are drawn to the occupation because of the **challenges** it presents to them daily. Occupational challenges can be somewhat standard and include:

- Shift work (with some shifts perhaps more stressful than others)
- Paramilitary structure
- Equipment deficiencies and shortages Paperwork perceived as unnecessary or excessive
- Lack of input into policy and decision making
- Lack of career development opportunities, with resulting competition among employees for the few available openings
- Lack of adequate training or supervision
- Lack of reward/recognition for efforts
- Role conflict
- Irregular work schedule
- Additional stress for female and ethnic minority employees:
    a. lack of acceptance by a predominately white, male police force with subsequent denial of information, alliances, and protection

b. lack of role models and mentors

c. pressure to prove oneself

d. lack of influence in decision making

- Court rulings perceived as too lenient on offenders
- Court rulings perceived as too restrictive on methods of criminal suppression and investigation
- Anxiety over the responsibility to protect others
- Disappointment when high expectations are not met
- Fear of doing something against regulations or being second-guessed

KEY TWO

The second key is that of **choice**. We are the only animals on the planet that choose what we become. This we know to be an unarguable fact. Each of us will share the same twenty-four hours in any given day, assuming we are fortunate enough to wake up and experience the day at all. Yes, it is a fact that life will go on. Whether it goes on with us or without us remains to be seen; whether we enjoy our lives is very often a choice.

It has been said the heart and the brain do not age. It seems, however, that if we do not use the latter to our best advantage, the former will eventually stop... prematurely.

While we may blame others for our current occupation, position, financial status, and more, we are actually the product of the choices we have made in life. Among the many choices we make every day, our attitudes are the most important. Your attitude will determine your altitude. Positive attitudes are always in the possession of positive people, while those who choose to be negative possess negative attitudes. No one is either positive or negative all the time; yet, it is where we spend most of the time that determines our destinies.

Among our many choices are:

- Whom we date
- Whom we marry
- Whether or not to have children
- The type of job we seek
- The job we finally accept
- How we see ourselves in that job
- Whether or not to seek promotion
- Seeking a transfer
- Getting bitter or getting better
- Seeking revenge or forgiving
- Blaming others or taking responsibility for our actions
- Honoring the people we work for
- Respecting our office
- Seeking new friendships

KEY THREE

The third key is the one that seems to be elusive. This key is that of change. Ironically, **change** is constant. When ladies get their hair curled, it is called a "permanent." Unfortunately, they are required to get a permanent every six months, proving that it is in fact not permanent, but temporary and subject to change. Change is ongoing in nature and should be ongoing in you. Assess your position in life, your attitudes, your likes and dislikes. Determine who relies on you and if you act responsibly. Decide to change and then simply do it.

Each of us possesses the ability to change. We can change the way we look through a change in hair style or other alteration on the outside, or we can change on the inside. It doesn't require any equipment. It just requires a commitment from you to view life differently and change behaviors. If you always do what you've always done, you'll always be what you've always been. The only ingredients for change are you and your goals. As Aristotle stated, "Without change there would be no need for time."

KEY FOUR

Key number four is that of **courage**. Courage is doing what you believe in. Early in my career, I learned that working cases with the FBI, together with state and local law enforcement, usually required stopping for a beer on the way home. I was new to the area, and to the office. I continually chose not to join them. I chose instead to go home, to be with my new bride. The others continued to go to the bars. I had no objection to what they chose to do.

There were a few who approached me and indicated that my lack of desire to join them for a drink reflected a lack of commitment to the office and left them with the impression I did not like the people I worked with. I assured them it had nothing to do with whether I liked them. Rather, it related directly to my wanting to go home at the end of the day and spend time with my wife. I chose to exercise my rights to live by my rules, not theirs. It always takes a certain amount of courage to be different. I had made a commitment to my wife. I am pleased to say that I continued to go home to my wife and daughter, and I still do.

Approximately three months after this incident, one of the individuals who had confronted me regarding my not drinking with them approached me and said, "Thanks." I asked him what for. He replied, "No one stops for drinks anymore." I told him that was their choice and that all I was doing was what I had committed to do. He interrupted and said it was my example that led the others to quit the habit of stopping each night. He said my behavior made the others stop and think. More importantly, he said that his son approached him the night before and told him, "Gee, Dad, you don't smell like beer anymore." It would appear he had established some rules in his life and put his family first. It paid off, and it always will. Perhaps your courage will inspire others.

The rules of life vary with every individual. Challenges are always present in trying to apply the rules to life. The rules by which I live my life are (1) Nothing comes before the God I believe in, and (2) I try to avoid knowingly doing anything that will bring dishonor to my family. Humans are far from perfect, but rules at least help us stay focused. Discover the rules in your life. If you come up empty-handed, create some. Share your rules with someone you care about.

KEY FIVE

Key number five is that of **control.** Learn to live in the present. Take calculated risks in efforts to improve your well-being. The greatest mistake a person can make is to be afraid of making one. Don't lament about what could have been. It's up to you to recapture control.

Regarding control, there is a certain caterpillar, the Pine Processionary Caterpillar *(Thaumetopoea pityocampa)* (Web.cortland.edu/fitzgerald/PineProcessio nary.html) that instinctively follows the caterpillar in front of it. Much like the caterpillar, we must ask, "Whom are we following?" and "Are they going where we want to be?"

KEY SIX

Commitment is the last of the six keys. Without this key, the others are subject to being left incomplete. This we know to be an unarguable fact. A commitment is an investment of your will. It usually requires that you give up some old habits that have not served you well. I recall having a student enter my office at the FBI Academy. He asked me if I had a few minutes and I stated that I had as much time as he needed. We had been talking for about twenty minutes when he blurted out, "I'm forty-three years of age and I am not where I want to be!" I then asked him where he wanted to be at forty-three and he replied, "I don't know." I simply said, "It appears as if you made it!" We spoke for the remainder of his time in the Academy about goal-setting. You can't achieve a goal you don't have, any more than you can hit a target you can't see. Your goals must be decided and then acted upon. The world doesn't care if you are successful. You must make that commitment yourself.

Be certain to write your goals down and review them from time to time. Goals should have the following components: A goal should be measurable, achievable, personal, and specific (MAPS). I had no expectations of receiving help from anyone upon my decision to retire from the FBI. Neither should you. Help is nice to have but you must be ready to stand alone should help not arrive. Thus a commitment is essential. I have had fun facing the challenges associated with building my company. I continue to enjoy providing training and consultation to the corporate sector, as well as providing informational and motivational presentations before law enforcement audiences throughout the world.

Together these keys—challenge, choice, change, courage, control, and commitment—can greatly assist us in recapturing command of our lives, allowing us to love our families more and serve our communities best.

9

POLICE LIFE PERSPECTIVE: WHICH WAY FROM HERE?

"FOR A SHIP WITH NO PORT, ANY WIND WILL GET IT THERE" (PARAPHRASED).

LUCIUS ANNAEUS SENECA, A ROMAN STOIC PHILOSOPHER (ca. 4 BC–AD 65)

There are more than three quarters of a million (750,000) police officers in the United States today. Law enforcement is a highly stressful job where an officer faces the effects of murder, violent assaults, accidents, and personal injury. More than seventy-five thousand police officers are assaulted each year on the job—more than two hundred officers a day. Unlike any other occupation, police officers are expected to die for the community they serve. It is an occupational hazard.

They are expected to risk their lives every day to protect the citizens who often do not appreciate their service. As a result, law enforcement families are expected to face on a daily basis the fear of loss and the sacrifice of their spouses. Police officers coping with the dregs of society are often forced to become comfortable with anger and sometimes dark humor to balance that. Law enforcement officers may be less comfortable with tenderness, displays of affection, and emotionality. Often they may replace requests with demands.

For instance, an officer might order his or her child, "Buckle up your seatbelt, or we are not going anywhere," as a result of habits from work. What motivates this show of anger is that the officer cannot relate to the child after experiencing stories of dead children pulled from car wrecks. The officer cannot communicate to the child how frightening is the thought this could happen to his or her own child. Police officers know that bad things happen to good people—not just to strangers but to good, everyday people.

Do we continue to deny the fact it may be the officer, and not solely the profession of law enforcement, that weakens existing interpersonal relationships? Does the profession prohibit the creation of new relationships? Is it fair to blame the job for all the shortcomings in our relationships with our families and friends? Can some law enforcement officers do their job well and still have a rewarding home life, while others fail? It seems that the overriding variable with regard to success and failure is the officer himself.

At the risk of oversimplifying a very dynamic and intricate problem, there is clearly only one direction we can take: acceptance of shortcomings or of inappropriate behaviors, followed by correction.

Taking responsibility for successful relationships is an individual duty. Blaming others for your problems is ineffective, at best, for obtaining solutions. Each of us has made mistakes. I (Reese) have had the pleasure and great opportunity to hear the Reverend R.T. Kendall preach. He states in his book Controlling the Tongue (2007) that "Holiness is achieved, little by little, not in proportion to our denying sin but in proportion to our coming to terms with its existence—in ourselves" (p. 51). The Scriptures teach us, "If we say that we have no sin, we deceive ourselves, and the truth is not in us" (1 John 1:8). We must accept the following facts:

- The profession of law enforcement is like none other with regard to stress, pressure, and the life-or-death demands experienced almost daily.
- The profession of law enforcement does not lend itself to gaining pity or sympathy from the public.
- The stress experienced by law enforcement personnel is a unique form of stress, requiring innovative stress management techniques.
- Those outside the profession have trouble identifying with police issues.
- Families are all but ignored by law enforcement agencies and are not regarded as the "ultimate backup."

- Police officers are reluctant to admit fault and/or seek help.

THE INNER WINNER

All serious daring starts from within. It simply isn't productive to blame the job or others for issues in life. While it may be true, it fails to solve problems. There comes a time when each officer must take a good look within. This introspective examination may be painful, but it is necessary if we don't want the public, friends, and family to start isolating themselves from us. There is a note of caution necessary here. Your introspective examination must be an honest one. Often, we are so used to being who we are that we fail to see how we've changed. We need a reminder from a loved one regarding who we are, who we were, and even who we could become.

This job will change you. What do you see changing? Are you more sarcastic, paranoid, cynical, isolated, judgmental, opinionated, and closed-minded? You may wish to ask your spouse or partner, "What do you see changing in me? In us?" Time away from family won't solve these issues. Discussions with family members are the beginning step. One must be willing to listen to the other person and share the responsibility for a healthy relationship.

After experiencing everything from pain to joy, insults to commendations, we become exhausted. Unable to argue, or take a stance that is opposed to those for whom we work, we bring the perceived injustice(s) home. It has been said by many officers and in many different ways, "If I can't win at work, I'll just have to wait until I get home."

Unfortunately, in order for one to win, most often another must lose. This is counterproductive to an active and healthy family lifestyle. For many officers, winning is everything, whether at work or at home. The concept can be clarified in this way. When we argue at home, it involves those we love. If we win, they must lose. We should be trying to make our loved ones feel like winners, not losers.

An important fact to remember is that arguments will occur in the best of relationships. As a husband, I have learned that, if I am wrong, I should be man enough to admit *I'm wrong*. And if I am right, I should be man enough to admit I'm wrong! This certainly holds true when the argument is about something meaningless. Often, it is just one partner trying to recapture self-esteem and control after a horrendous day.

Not until we have received advanced training in interrogation or negotiation do we learn about "win-win" options. It seems these skills could be taught in our academies for use with everyday family issues and then applied to work. Win-win should not be exclusive to our occupation.

Law enforcement officers work a good job and a rewarding one for the most part. Although the negative aspects of the job are often highlighted, no one should ever doubt the positive attitudes of most law enforcement officers and the love they have for their jobs and their families. The value of law enforcement officers in our society can not be underestimated. Societies can not succeed where policing fails. Similarly, families can not succeed where individual officers fail to see the need to monitor their feelings, and properly balance their time and resources.

Our careers lead us down a path of "exactness" with no allowance for the occasional mistake. It is either legal or illegal. There is no "wiggle room" as might be found in other professions. While the public may make distinctions between logical and illogical, moral and immoral, right and wrong, officers must enforce the law. It is either legal or illegal.

LOOK FOR SOLUTIONS

The recommendation to take steps to effectively manage stress and regain control of one's identity is frequently met with resistance. Just as there is some antipathy between so-called liberals and conservatives, there tends to be some suspiciousness, resistance, and negative feeling between mental health professionals and police officers. No one expects you to solve all your problems at one time. In fact, optimists continually look for partial solutions and to interrupt negative thoughts. They don't take everything personally and are able to celebrate the success of others.

One major reason for resistance on the part of officers is the notion that they (consciously or unconsciously) associate stress management with the need for personal assistance and a lessening of their police image, making them feel more vulnerable. There is a conflict between managing the excessive stress and their attraction to the excitement of police work.

Still others may think stress management serves to "soften" one's outlook and therefore lessens one's ability to confront danger. Fortunately, learning to manage stress and increase family satisfaction does not teach one to become uninvolved and easygoing. Rather, one learns how to appropriately react when confronted with stressful situations, and how to take relatively nonstressful situations in stride. It allows us to have more time for family. Just like athletes are expected to react in certain ways based upon the situations they find themselves in, so too are other professionals such as law enforcement officers. The true professional has the opportunity to react intentionally to situations, rather than unintentionally (Reese and Bright, 1987).

Law enforcement families unite at work and at home to optimize an officer's productivity and wellness. My husband (Castellano) was assigned long hours on a job that kept him working for more than seventy consecutive days. Exhausted and lonely, both he and I had been discussing how difficult it was for all of us, when a letter arrived for me in the mail (see Appendix B). It was from his commanding officer, thanking me for my sacrifices and support during this important initiative. The letter went on to say that my sacrifices had allowed my spouse and the unit to successfully execute arrests and complete the job, making our community and state better places. Tears rolled down my cheeks as I read the letter, amazed that anyone noticed I was trying to do my part to help my husband "catch the bad guys," as my seven-year-old would explain. The letter made up for the times I felt invisible in the process while trying to silently support my partner and his public service. I saved the letter, and will cherish it, as it validated my commitment to serve my husband as a police officer's wife, energized to be without him another seventy days if need be. It was a "happy ending" to a difficult time in our law enforcement family.

10

BLESSED ARE THE PEACEMAKERS; FOR THEY SHALL BE CALLED THE CHILDREN OF GOD *(Matthew 5:9)*

PUTTING IT ALL TOGETHER; AND KEEPING IT ALL TOGETHER.

Among the many purposes of this book has been to dispel a number of myths surrounding law enforcement families, from the rituals of an officer not being able to share his feelings, to the taboos created by officers' children needing to be "better" than other children. Another purpose was to offer some remedies. Hopefully, after reading this book, readers will be able to take a calmer, more objective look at their relationships and the issues they face.

For some, obstacles are merely challenges for growth. For others, they are an ever-present excuse for not achieving happiness. Why is it that one officer can have a wonderful and rewarding career, a loving family, and reasonable debts, be spiritually well, and be addiction-free, while his partner, riding in the same cruiser, hates his job, lost his family, drinks to excess, and has a troublesome debt load? The question remains, "What are the elements and/or influences that cause one to be a success and another to be a dismal failure when there are no obvious differences in them or their circumstances?" We believe it may center, in many cases, on the choices one makes in life. Yes, we are aware that circumstances and events can "knock you to your knees." For some, that is devastating. For others, there is a realization little can be done in some circumstances and being on your knees means you won't lose your footing.

Regarding addictions, it can be argued some forms of addiction may be genetic and that people process stimuli differently. We would be naïve, if not ignorant, if we did not know this to be the case in some instances. What separates sobriety from addiction may be the choices each makes to cope with stress, and how they alter their attitudes, creating or eliminating counterproductive behaviors.

Our law enforcement academies often cite common police issues as alcohol abuse, suicide, and divorce. The triad permeates the thoughts of young recruits and their families. It seems if the recruits truly believed this would happen to them, they would leave the academy and seek another job. Why do they stay? Apparently because they believe these things happen to other people. They are taught that law enforcement encompasses long hours, time away from home, missed opportunities with family and friends, assignments ranging from dangerous to boring, and constant exposure to an ungrateful public. There is no basis for joy in these comments. In essence, law enforcement officers are programmed to expect to sacrifice a portion of their lives and time with family for the greater good.

This book teaches that an officer can have it all. A young officer should not be told to hope for the best but prepare for the worst, at least not in the context of family. It is a known fact this mentality is often appropriate for actual police work, but our personal environments can be manipulated and improved by caring officers— officers who don't just say they put their families first, but actually do. There are few things more depressing than a young pessimist.

Priorities are often illusive. We continually say our families come first, that the job is just a way to earn income, and that personal time is important. When asking law enforcement officers about their priorities, we hear "God, family, and friends." That sounds nice! But the follow-up questions reveal the shallowness of their commitment to their alleged priorities.

How often do you attend church? "Well, I can't always do that because I work shifts." Please understand that is not an answer to the question. The answer is often "seldom," if not "never." Many officers tend not to be involved deeply in their faith. Many will boldly state, based upon what they experience daily at work, they begin to doubt if people are, in fact, basically good; if there really is a "master plan." It pains them to say it but they have all but convinced themselves of the notion that the world rotates because of its 'lack of balance," not some divine plan.

Another question regards time spent together as a family. The question may be phrased, "When was your last real, planned vacation with the people you love?" Or, "When was the last time you spent quality time with your spouse, or children, or both?" Excuses range from a lack of time to a lack of money, yet many officers retire and collect money for "leave" days they have not used. It is known that many do not take vacation days so they can have this so-called "pot of gold" at the end of their career.

This only gives credence to the notion that people often do not live what they say they believe. People should be able to state succinctly what their priorities are and then demonstrate how they spend time on those priorities. If not, it's just a lot of talk, and it is a known fact that "talk is cheap."

Take an introspective look at yourself. Is there a positive correlation between the things that really matter to you and the time and effort you give them? Remember, life is not about balancing your abilities, but rather it is about your ability to balance. Finding time for the important things in life means you must identify them and then honor them.

All faiths are belief systems. Even those who choose not to believe in a supreme being have rules by which to live, from priorities to a moral compass. Perhaps a good exercise would be to find someone who knows you well and ask them, "What do you think my priorities are?" "What are the principles that guide my life?" The answers should reflect your stated values, but they may be shocking.

Too often officers believe stress and unhappiness are the price they must pay for success. But the most successful officers have a holistic view of their job and life. All human beings experience stress in one form or another. Some are exposed to it more than others. Some personally witnessed September 11th in New York City. Others heard about it in America's heartland on the television. Some had loved ones there. Others were detached and had no personal connections.

This book listed some of the unique sources of stress in law enforcement. This is not to say other jobs do not have unique stressors. People working in coal mines have stresses and fears different from those of bankers. Yet both must maintain balance in their lives. The fear must be overcome in order for them to make a living. This book suggests coping via reality, not denial. You simply have to want success more than you fear failure. For everything there is a season. There is a time to be a "sure-thing" taker, and times to be a risk taker. The challenges are those of choice and timing.

Cops and their families relate to issues and events affecting other cops and their families, regardless of where these events occur or if they are witnessed personally or via the media. When the news reports a police officer has been injured, every police officer, every law enforcement family member old enough to understand identifies immediately with the issues. We must understand that, with global and immediate communication, law enforcement as a whole, from practitioners to families, is instantly affected.

A purpose of this chapter is to confirm that it is acceptable, and allowable, to have faith and to demonstrate that faith in your life. "God bless America," "In God we trust"—these are the phrases on which America was built. For some, these phrases have become just that, simply words. The most recent United States one dollar piece has the phrase "In God We

Trust," but hidden on the edge of the coin. Well, many of us do not need that statement on our money to remind us of its validity.

The authors of this book are seriously committed believers in God. This too is a choice each of us must make. However, if you cannot identify with this concept, then consider the following guidelines and promises. If you cannot relate to a supreme being, you must find something stronger than yourself or you will be the only source of help you have. Throughout the Bible we read encouraging words and constructive directions, such as:

- Yea, though I walk through the valley of the shadow of death, I will fear no evil, for thou art with me. *(Psalm 23:4)*
- These things I command you, that ye love one another. *(John 15:17)*
- Judge not, that ye be not judged. *(Matthew 7:1)*

Turn difficult issues over to a greater power, and there is a chance the shortcomings in your life will change. Encouragement will replace despair, and hope will reign instead of self-pity. Understand that the natural man does not accept the things that come from the Spirit of God, because they are foolishness to him and he cannot understand them. Change what you think and you will change who you are.

The authors of this book are people of faith. We realize, and teach, that we become a product of what we spend most of our time thinking about. If you believe that spirituality is important, then focus on it.

What is the image of man? A man named Job asked, What is man that the Creator would be mindful of him? We are given independence, the ability and opportunity to think for ourselves. Our thoughts create our very being. Think about being depressed all day and the only option in your life is depression. Think about joy and the infinite possibilities available, and hope suddenly becomes your companion.

It goes without saying our society has been quite creative in providing us with an image of man. Unfortunately, this image revolves around a façade of material items that provide "status," as well as a "macho" image of toughness. This does not fit well in the true image of man. Unfortunately, these façades are what society cherishes. Look around you. We don't have to tell you where society is headed.

Among the greatest responsibilities facing men in this world is that of leadership. If American families are to survive the incredible stresses and dangers they now face, it will be because husbands and fathers provide loving and ethical leadership in their homes, placing their wives and children second only to the God they believe in on their list of priorities. Unfortunately, it seems more difficult to teach proper values today than in years past because of the widespread rejection of religious principles in our culture. While there is an apparent disregard for the moral standards of the Bible, it doesn't mean they can't be taught.

It is possible for mothers and fathers to love and revere God while systematically losing their children. You can go to church three times a week, serve on the governing body, attend meetings, give your money, and make all the right "religious noises" yet fail to communicate what spirituality actually means.

The complete absence of love can destroy one emotionally, and sometimes physically. An infant who is not loved, touched, or caressed will often die. Prussian king Frederick II conducted an experiment with fifty infants in the thirteenth century. He wanted to know what language the infants would speak if they never heard the spoken word. Foster mothers bathed and suckled the children but were forbidden to cuddle or talk to the infants. He never learned what he wanted to know because all fifty infants died (Halsall, 2006).

Relay races are won or lost in the transfer of the baton. Rarely is the baton dropped when placed firmly in the runner's grasp. Putting the Truth, the Gospel, safely in the hands of our children is crucial. Our number one responsibility is to evangelize our own children. Based upon the current trends in the "real world," they will not learn "the Truth" out there.

Life is not a scrimmage, it is our Super Bowl. It is the only game in town. The Super Bowl we watch on TV is timed. Everyone knows when it will be over. In the game of life, God is the timekeeper and he does not share with us how long our game will last. It is serious business. The question is, "Are you willing to take the chance that you have plenty of time?" "Is your image of man suitable for a spiritually strong life and family?"

In the world today, law enforcement officers are needed more than ever. No one seems to want to be honest and play by the rules. It is important to remember that peacemakers, who sow in peace, reap a harvest of goodness. Why is spirituality important? The Spirit of God is ever-present, abundant, comforting, and everlasting. Nothing else on Earth offers those promises. Here are the steps:

1. Be made right with the Creator you believe in. By placing your faith in a power (the Power) stronger than your own, you can rely on help in time of need that far surpasses any skills or talents you may have.

2. Let that peace be ever-present in your heart and actions. Give your Creator first place in your life, and acknowledge Him for all you are and have.

3. Fix your thoughts on what is good. By thinking of what is true, and good, and right, we escape the temptations of negative thoughts.

4. Admit there are many things you can correct in your life. A good confession to oneself is healthy and revealing. It's time to stop carrying the baggage of guilt around with us for past deeds. Correct them and move on! Forgiving is for giving (to yourself, too)!

5. Resist associations that will bring evil and condemnation to bear upon you. In many respects you, in fact, will be judged by the company you keep, because they influence your behavior.

6. Leave the past behind you. As humans, we seem to have a need to reflect on past failures and impose self-condemnation. You will not know where you are going if you are looking behind you. Your eyes were placed in the front of your head because where you are going is far more important than where you have been.

7. Be the example. Let family, friends, and co-workers see the real you. Set your standards high and then maintain those standards. It doesn't matter where you have been. Today is a new day and you can be

a new creature. Chart your course well. Your future, from this time forward and into eternity, is important. While you cannot predict your future, spiritual priorities will assist you in influencing it.

8. Our spouses and children rely on our guidance as parents and guardians. Begin to act responsibly. As for your children, train them in the way they should go, and when they are old, they will not depart from it (Proverbs 22:6).

"The Lord works in mysterious ways, often beyond human understanding. When people try to figure out how God works in the inner man and transforms a person, they can easily fall into psychological speculation. The Lord truly transforms people, but he does it through His Word, His Spirit, and His Body. When it comes to understanding human nature and how people change, why not trust in the Lord and His Word alone and lean not unto psychological speculation?" (Missler, 1996).

Police officers work in a world where there is constant struggle between good and evil. More than any other public service profession, those in the field of law enforcement are in a unique position to make a spiritual difference in the lives of both co-workers and citizens they encounter. However, without a firm spiritual foundation, the stress found in a law enforcement career can drag an officer down. Once again we turn to our faith to be raised up in this journey of public service. May you be blessed with the joy you so richly deserve by your family and your career. Proverbs 12:20 explains "Deceit is in the heart of them that imagine evil, but to the counselors of peace is joy." The authors of this book wish you peace...always.

APPENDIX A

GUIDELINES FOR LAW ENFORCEMENT FAMILIES
IN DISASTER

1. **Prepare beforehand.** Consider in your law enforcement family, "What would we do if . . .?" Have a family night discussion in which you describe scenarios regarding natural, man-made, even bioterrorism disasters. What is the family disaster plan? Who can help the law enforcement family when your officer may be out in the community assisting others? How will you establish communication to confirm that your plan has been executed properly?

2. **Accentuate the positive.** Identify and acknowledge that although as a law enforcement family you may face a crisis or disaster, this experience may allow you together to gain positive intimacy and recognize your resilience. This will minimize anxiety in reviewing the plan.

3. **Walk a day in my shoes.** Perhaps when officers on elite rescue teams or units get deployed to disasters outside our area, officer and spouse lose empathy for each other. By walking a day in the other's shoes, a husband and wife can change roles and traditional

tasks. He can handle the kids and dinner at home, while she empathizes through perhaps photographs, descriptions of duties, even details of rescue and recovery missions to appreciate what her husband experienced on deployment. This may foster "mutual aid" within your family.

4. **Get out of the rut.** After a traumatic event or disaster you may feel out of your routine. Embrace it! Deliberately let new experiences occur. Create a new focus, a hobby, a volunteer activity to shift both of you away from the trauma or remnants of the disaster you have survived.

5. **Humor.** Law enforcement officers often survive traumatic events by coping using "dark humor." Have a family funny night. Although in times of crisis it sometimes seems awkward or even impossible to laugh, you can allow yourself to relax. It is imperative for your survival.

6. **Store strength.** Get back to basics. Be prepared in specific ways. Store food and water, and have safety drills and three months' salary tucked away just in case a disaster keeps you apart. Understand and know that your officer and the family both have mechanisms for survival for an extended period of time. A sense of security in basic survival needs will promote confidence in your family.

7. **Remind yourselves of what you used to do together.** Enjoy together. Surviving tragedy or crisis can often reroute us from our passions and loves, our hobbies, and things that define who we are. Try to do those things together as a family or a couple. Perhaps you can try fishing together, or even doing yoga, going to the gym, or something that allows you to play together rather than just survive. Just enjoy being together.

8. **Communicate.** Crisis and disaster can prompt an officer to function on "autopilot." Communicate not just around logistics and specifics. Get back to loving language, talking about your renewed faith and rewritten core beliefs. Encourage family discussions now more than ever.

9. **Pray together.** Law enforcement families and couples often rely on their faith as a foundation. Praying together is imperative for success. Crisis can be an opportunity to develop your faith.

10. **Encourage each other.** Lack of control and helplessness in disasters can lead officers to a unique sense of vulnerability. Encourage each other's strengths in order to reaffirm your love. With the strength, make a bombardment of actions to renew the love between husband and wife. Our

perceptions as men and women are different. We may think we are being loving but somehow miss the mark, particularly when we are out of our routines and perhaps not in touch with each other's needs.

Even our children have expectations of how we should show our love and often we miss those opportunities. For example, as a mom (Castellano) I may say "I love you" to my son. But perhaps my love would be demonstrated best by playing catch with him on the front lawn on a sunny afternoon.

APPENDIX B

LETTER FROM A SUPERVISOR

Dear Cherie,

2005 is quickly coming to an end and so too is another year of work completed by the men and women of the Special Enforcement Unit. This was an especially challenging year, as we took on a number of complex cases with unusual and oftentimes bizarre circumstances. While the work that is produced in this Unit is of a confidential nature, it's no secret that this Unit prides itself on maintaining the best and brightest professionals in the law enforcement and legal community to produce results such as those we have enjoyed in 2005. [Your husband] Mark is no exception.

It has been said that this work is not only a choice but a calling. It cannot be overstated that while our commitment and duty to serve and protect the most vulnerable in our community is the driving force behind the work we do, it comes with a price. The sacrifices endured by dedicated community servants, such as Mark, pales in comparison to the sacrifices of the family members who support our work. But for your love, support, and understanding of Mark, we could not realize the profound and positive results of those sacrifices. For that, I wish to express my deepest gratitude to you and your entire family. You are as much a part of this team as any other and your support of Mark is the foundation which makes the mission possible. Thank you."

Sincerely,
Jeffrey S. Paul,
Captain, Tactical Operations

APPENDIX C

COPS DON'T CRY (STONE, 1999)

THE FAMILY LAW ENFORCEMENT CODE OF ETHICS

The Family Law Enforcement Code of Ethics is a guide to ensure stronger family ties. As the family of an officer, part of our fundamental duty is to work together to help safeguard the family's well-being so the officer may return home and recover his sense of perspective.

We will do this by providing a loving and relaxed environment so he feels welcome and appreciated. We will make an effort to communicate so we may understand each other's hardships and work together to solve them.

We will recognize that this lifestyle is "different" and accept it as a positive challenge, being constantly mindful of each other's welfare. We will see each other without judgment and become our own best self so we may create a strong relationship with unquestioned trust and understanding.

We will strive to find some sense of order in the disorder, self-appreciation in times of loneliness, creativity in chaos, and time to be together when there's never any time.

We will not insult the officer's choice of profession by selfishly demonstrating our personal feelings toward something he can't change.

We will understand that he takes his commitment to the job very seriously.

Officers are constantly under pressure to uphold their private lives as an example to others and as a family we will also strive to uphold those beliefs.

We recognize that living with a police officer can be extremely trying but we will wear our invisible badge with commitment and pride, and ride the wave of excitement and realism with him throughout his career.

We will always strive to achieve these objectives and ideals, dedicating ourselves before God to help the officer do his very best in his chosen profession . . . law enforcement.

APPENDIX D

You can accomplish most of your dreams if you take the right steps. How successful you become, whether in terms of a paycheck or happiness, will depend largely on how well you plan.

Areas to Think About in Writing a Career or Life Plan

- What are your long-term goals?
- What are your short-term goals?
- What obstacles or "roadblocks" are preventing you from reaching those goals?

How Do You Start?

- Your written career plan can be as simple as two or three pages of notes, or very detailed. The more detailed the better.
- Devise a goal-oriented plan by breaking the goals down into categories to keep track of your progress.
- Goals should include all the steps needed to conquer" them.
- Having a plan for your life and your career will demand that you do enough research to stay abreast of the job market.

- Be inventive.
- Consider all possible trails to blaze even if some of the alternatives don't comply with your immediate desires.

Strategies for Evaluating More Alternatives—Think in terms of being an entrepreneur

- Keep your priorities straight.
- Daydreaming is extremely important.

Getting Down to Business

- Write down at least three long-term goals and three short-term goals.
- It is important to have everything on paper so you won't be relying on memory alone on a regular basis to propel yourself forward.

Consider Your Family's Needs

- By writing down your goals and assessing how they'll impact your family, you can strategize your moves to cause the least upheaval in your personal life.

What to Do to Motivate Yourself to Act

- Network continually.
- Talk with anyone and everyone who will share how he or she made a career climb.
- Go online to chat in discussion groups.

- Talk with counselors at your local college.
- Attend a career-planning seminar.
- Go to conferences.
- Make a list of the activities you have enjoyed during the past few years.
- Evaluate why you enjoy participating in these activities.
- Write down the skills you possess. Include "people skills," good communication skills, and problem-solving skills, along with your medical expertise.
- Write down a few career choices and pencil in the benefits of each choice.
- Make a list of professional journals, magazines, and newsletters you need to read and where you could obtain copies.
- Develop and maintain a professional portfolio documenting your work and related accomplishments.

APPENDIX E

1. Know thyself.

The stress of police work and response can induce a state of psychological uncertainty, personal vulnerability, frustration, and even demoralization for all affected. The mental health of the officer fighting crime is a crucial resource in the fight. To understand normal and more severe reactions will serve one well in the daily struggle. Differentiating the "benign" from the "malignant" psychological symptoms is essential. Specialized training in "target-hardening," stress resistance, and stress resiliency may serve as a form of psychological "body armor" for law enforcement professionals and their families. Decide what works for your entire family to be resilient, and do it regularly!

2. Know thy enemy as you know thyself. (Sun Tzu)

While it is essential to know oneself—strengths, weaknesses, normal reactions, more severe reactions— it is also essential to know the enemy. Perhaps the enemy is the criminal on the street, maybe it is a boss due to management difficulty, or even another officer on your job. The strengths, weaknesses, and understanding of who and why you are labeling an enemy may provide insight into your future behavior and success. Misdirected anger and emotions can confound who and what we are fighting about and for. Know the enemy in your family, community, and workplace, and stay focused on resolution.

3. And he shall lead them.

"Crisis leadership" skills are a unique form of leadership seldom taught in traditional leadership classes. They are essential in building a comprehensive psychological resilience. Crisis leadership aims to foster productivity while encouraging recognition of emotional and psychological implications of the job. The goal is to maximize productivity of the workforce within units or agencies. Grief leadership skills, suicide prevention and awareness, and substance abuse issues, as well as practical applications pertaining to policy and logistics, should be reviewed. Skills in crisis communications are an important aspect of crisis leadership. Family leadership is established to foster a close unit that achieves the goal of a happy home.

4. It was then that I carried you . . .

Establish psychological support initiatives utilizing crisis intervention hotlines, outreach personnel, and crisis centers as needed. Given that the exposure of human suffering is unprecedented in the field of police work, any resource directed to support psychological health may not only be seen as fostering health, but may be seen as fostering national defense. Employee assistance programs, union organizations, local hospitals, and health plans must offer resources that can enhance resiliency and foster recovery. Don't forget to enlist spiritual and faith-based resources in any intervention program.

Finally, psychological first aid should be taught as readily as physical first aid. Family members may take turns carrying each other to have an optimal experience in support and love.

5. Honor thy family.

For police officers, family is the first line of aid and support. But the family is not only a source of support—it may inadvertently become a target for expressed frustrations. The increased tours of duty, danger, chaos, and uncertainty in one's own life can get transferred to family members, depleting their ability to provide support, as well as making them tertiary victims. Family discord, family violence, and divorce may be seen to increase as stress increases. Your family is a priority that cannot be neglected without consequence. Family support groups, printed materials and Web sites, spiritual activities, and family counseling may be necessary on a regular or intermittent basis to provide support and strengthen that imperative resource.

6. Be Your Brother's Keeper.

Foster the creation and maintenance of your brotherhood and sisterhood in law enforcement. Beware that your police family does not replace your family of origin. Use your closeness and unity to look out for each other. Practice techniques like question, persuade, and refer (QPR), which in essence is an awareness of a fellow officer's suicidal risk or decompensation. Keep your eyes wide open at home too, as your family may need interventions to save one another throughout your lives.

7. Foster the familiar.

Reestablish normal communication, transportation, and economic, educational, and work schedules as soon as possible after a critical incident or stressor at work. There is safety in the familiar. The greater the disruption to normal routines, the greater the perceived adversity. Encourage your family to be "guilt-free" in the pursuit of happiness after a tragedy.

8. Honor the living and the dead—the cross at Ground Zero.

Utilize the power of symbols as a means of reestablishing cohesion. Flags, signs, patriotic slogans, and other symbols can create a universal experience and connection among units, agencies, and civilians. Most public safety personnel do not seek recognition but instead shy away from accolades, as humility is a common quality among them. It is imperative to allow for recognition and acknowledgment. Ceremonies, symbols, and rituals of closure are for many an essential aspect of healing and recovery.

9. Start Anew.

At times, there will be a need to move an officer and his family, organization, community, or nation ahead after some experiences on the job by creating a new epoch or era of rebirth . . . "a new beginning." Return to "normal" life after traumatic events may be difficult, as regular life may be perceived as mundane. In the past a "Psychological Reentry Program" has been successfully used to facilitate this process for law enforcement personnel (Castellano, 2003). Law enforcement families can re-create themselves as units and as individuals when tragedy becomes an opportunity to reassess in this time period.

10. That which does not kill me makes me stronger. (Nietzsche)

Positive outcomes and growth can occur for some who are exposed to trauma (Tedeschi and Calhoun, 1996).

After exposure to trauma, an opportunity to experience oneself as better may arise in three areas: personal awareness, spiritual growth, and family resolutions. Not everyone needs psychological services after a traumatic event! Family bonds are strengthened for most optimists.

REFERENCES

Bailey, F. Lee. 1971. *The defense never rests.* With H. Aronson. New York: Stein & Day.

Bartolome, F. 1983. The work alibi, when it's harder to go home, *Harvard Business Review.*

Bibbins, V. 1986. The quality of family and marital life of police personnel. In Reese, J., and H. Goldstein, eds, *Psychological services for law enforcement.* Government Printing Office: Washington, DC, 423.

Brewin, C., and E. Holmes. 2003. Psychological theories of posttraumatic stress disorder, *Clinical Psychology Review* (UK) 23:339–76.

Carte, G., and E. Carte, Police reform in the United States: *The era of August Vollmer,*1975. Berkeley: University of California Press, 26. Quoted in Gladis, S. 1985. The FBI National Academy's first fifty fears, *FBI Law Enforcement Bulletin,* July, 2.

Castellano, C. 2003. Large group crisis intervention for law enforcement in response to the September 11 World Trade Center mass disaster. *International Journal of Emergency Mental Health* 5:211–15.

References

_____, J. Nestor, and L. Mascioli. 2005. Psychological first aid for first responders, *Journal of Counterterrorism & Homeland Security* 10, no. 2.

_____, W. Ussery, and S. Gruntfest. 2006. Looking for higher ground post-Katrina. *Journal of Counterterrorism & Homeland Security* 12, no. 2.

Cramer, J. 1964. *The World's Police.* London: Cassell and Company Ltd, 4406.

Denevi, D., J. Campbell, S. Bond, and J. Otto. 2004. *Into the minds of madmen: How the FBI's Behavioral Science Unit revolutionized crime investigation.* New York: Prometheus Books.

Depue, R. 1981. The high-risk lifestyle: The police family. *FBI Law Enforcement Bulletin* 50, no. 8 (August).

Encyclopedia Britannica. Anna Freud. http://www.britannica.com/eb/article-9035389 (accessed July 3, 2007).

Everly, G., and C. Castellano. 2005. *Psychological counterterrorism and World War IV.* Ellicott City, MD: Chevron Publishing.

Everly, G., and J. Reese. 2007. *Psychological body armor: Seven strategic lessons about life, resiliency, and coping with stress.* Ellicott City, MD: Chevron Publishing.

Figley ,C. 1995. *Compassion fatigue: Secondary traumatic stress disorders. In Those who treat the traumatized, Psychosocial Stress book series.* England: Routledge.

Freud, Anna. 1936. *Ego and Mechanisms of Defense.*

Freud, Sigmund. (1894). The neuro-psychoses of defence. SE 3, 41–61.

Friedman, C. 2005. *Spiritual Survival for Law Enforcement.* Linden, NJ: Compass Books.

Hartsough, D., and D. Myers. 1985. *Disaster work and mental health: Prevention and control of stress among workers.* Washington, DC: National Institute of Mental Health, Center for Mental Health Studies for Emergencies.

Holy Bible, King James Version. 1974. Dallas, TX: International Bible Association.

Hooker, R. 1996. Pietas Respect for Authority. http://www.wsu.edu:8080/~dee/GLOSSARY/PIETAS.HTM (accessed July 2007).

Kadish, S., ed. 1983. *Encyclopedia of crime and justice.* London: Collier Macmillan Publishers, 3:1211.

Kendall, R. 2007. *Controlling the tongue.* Lake Mary, FL: Charisma Publishing House.

Kessler, R. 2002. *The Bureau: The secret story of the FBI.* New York: St. Martin's Press.

Kirschman, E. 1997 and 2000. *I Love a Cop.* New York and London: Guilford Press.

Mann, P. 1980. Ethical issues for psychologists in police agencies. *In Who is the client?*, ed. J. Monahan. Washington, DC: American Psychological Association, 18.

Maslow, A. 1943. A theory of human motivation. *Psychological Review* 50, no. 4.

Missler, N. 1996. Nancy Missler & psychoheresy, part 2: Missler responds. www.psychoheresy-aware.org/missler2 (accessed July 3, 2007).

Niederhoffer, A., and E. Niederhoffer. 1978. *The police family—from the station house to the ranch house.* Lexington, MA: Lexington Books.

Patire, T. 2003. *Personal protection handbook.* New York: Three Rivers Press.

Paton, D., and J. Violanti. 2006. Who gets PTSD?: *Issues of post traumatic stress vulnerability.* Springfield, IL: Charles C. Thomas.

Pine processionary caterpillar. Web.cortland.edu/fitzgerald/PineProcessionary.html (accessed July 2, 2007).

Reese, J. 1988. Psychological aspects of policing violence. In Reese, J., and J. Horn. *Police psychology: Operational Assistance.* Washington, DC: U.S. Department of Justice, FBI, 347–63.

_____, 1987. The History of the Development of Psychological Services in Law Enforcement Organizations in the United States. Dissertation abstracts.

_____, 1987. *The History of Police Psychological Services.* Washington, DC: Federal Bureau of Investigation.

_____, Forthcoming. *Six Keys to Stress Free Living.* Williamsburg, VA: Richmond Hill Press.

_____, and D. Bright. 1982. Stress management: A proactive approach. *The National Sheriff,* June–July.

References

_____, J. Horn, and C. Dunning, eds. 1991. *Critical incidents in policing, rev.* Washington, DC: U.S. Department of Justice, FBI.

_____, and E. Scrivner, eds. 1991. *The law enforcement family: Issues and Answers.* Washington, DC: U.S. Department of Justice, FBI.

Reiser, M. 1972. *The police department psychologist.* Springfield, IL: Charles C. Thomas.

_____, 1986. James Reese telephone interview with Director, Behavioral Science Services, Los Angeles Police Department. Los Angeles, CA, July 30.

Russell, H., and A. Beigel. 1991. *Understanding human behavior for effective police work.* New York: Basic Books.

Satir, V., J. Banmen, J. Gerber, and M. Gormin. 1991. *The Satir model: Family therapy and beyond.* Palo Alto, CA: Science and Behavior Books.

Seal, M., and J. Speziale. 2003. *Without a badge: Undercover in the world's deadliest criminal organization.* New York: Kensington Books.

Stone, V. 1999. *Cops Don't Cry.* Ottawa, Canada: Creative Bound.

Stratton, J. 1984. *Police Passages*. Manhattan Beach, CA: Glennon Publishing.

Stritof, S. and B. Marriage Tips. http://marriage.about.com/mbiopage:html (accessed July 3, 2007).

Tavris, C.,1982. Anger: *The misunderstood emotion*. New York: Simon and Schuster, 37.

Tedeschi, R., and L. Calhoun. 1996. The post-traumatic growth inventory. *Journal of Traumatic Stress* 9:455–71.

U.S. House of Representatives. 1991. On the front lines: Police stress and family well-being. May 1991 hearing. Washington, DC: Government Printing Office.

Violanti, J. 1996. *Police Suicide*. Springfield, IL: Charles C. Thomas.

_____, C. Castellano, J. O'Rourke, and D. Paton. 2006. Proximity to the 9/11 terrorist attack and suicide ideation in police officers. *Traumatology* 12, no. 3.

Vollmer, A. 1921. Practical method for selecting policemen. *Journal of Criminal Law and Criminology* 12:571–81.

References

Wambaugh, J. 1987. *Echoes in the Darkness.* New York: Perigord Press.

Wyrick, M. 1966. Where Cops Came From. *The Wisconsin Police Chief* (December), 7.

ABOUT THE AUTHORS

Dr. Reese is a twenty-five-year veteran law enforcement officer, husband, and father. He has interviewed thousands of law enforcement officers in the past three decades regarding family issues, trauma, leadership issues, and stress. He is an award-winning author, lecturer, and consultant who holds a doctorate of philosophy. He has written the only *History of Psychological Services for Law Enforcement Officers in the United States* (1987). Dr. Reese worked fugitive, criminal, and foreign counterintelligence matters as a Supervisory Special Agent of the FBI and lectured at the FBI National Academy, Quantico, Virginia, for eighteen years. He was on the faculty of the Junior Command Course at Bramshill, Hampshire, England, under the command of Sir Kenneth Newman in 1982, and consulted with the Royal Ulster Constabulary (formerly the Royal Irish Constabulary and now known as the Police Service of Northern Ireland) and the British Police Home Office on post-shooting trauma in the early 1980s. He holds awards of excellence from the International Association of Chiefs of Police, The National Sheriffs' Association, the United States Department of Justice, NASA, The Director of the FBI, and others. While at the FBI Academy, he created the much-needed Stress Management in Law Enforcement (S.M.I.L.E.) course for the University of Virginia (university course number CJ 475), for use at the FBI Academy. An original FBI Criminal Personality Profiler, he retired from the FBI's Behavioral Science Unit (the unit portrayed in *Silence of the Lambs*) after profiling and interviewing criminals of all kinds, from serial killers to child molesters.

Dr. Reese served in the United States Army as a platoon leader in combat in Vietnam and was awarded the United States of America's Bronze Star Medal and the Republic of Vietnam's Distinguished Service Cross, together with other medals and awards.

He continues to write and provide lectures worldwide as CEO of James T. Reese and Associates (www.jamestreese.com). He is a fellow of the American Academy of Experts in Traumatic Stress, a diplomat in police and criminal psychology with the Society for Police and Criminal Psychology, and proprietor of Richmond Hill Press LLC. He has edited and/or authored seven books, his latest entitled *Psychological Body Armor: Seven Strategic Lessons About Life, Resiliency, and Coping with Stress* (Everly & Reese, 2007).

Cherie Castellano is the Program Director of Cop2Cop at University Behavioral HealthCare, the first legislated law enforcement crisis hotline in the United States. She is a faculty member of the New Jersey Medical School Department of Psychiatry – University of Medicine and Dentistry of New Jersey. Mrs. Castellano has been recognized internationally as an expert in the field of behavioral health care and crisis intervention for law enforcement professionals. She has been a presenter at international forums in Australia and Europe, as well as at prestigious national venues such as the FBI National Academy.

Mrs. Castellano's programs in crisis intervention have been called "A Model for the Nation" by The New York Times. Additional awards include various New Jersey governors' proclamations, the New Jersey Governor's Excellence Award, the New Jersey Attorney General Recognition Award, and the International Critical Incident Stress Foundation World Congress's Award for Outstanding Response in Mass Disaster.

Following September 11th she was assigned to coordinate a critical-incident response to more than 1,900 first responders in New York and New Jersey. As a member of the 9/11 New York Emergency Service Delegation, Cherie traveled to Northern Ireland and

England to share "9/11 lessons learned." Cherie co-authored a critically acclaimed book entitled *Psychological Counterterrorism & World War IV* (Everly & Castellano, 2005) and has a regular column in *The Journal of Counterterrorism and Homeland Security International.*